GERHARD EBELING

Theology and Proclamation

Dialogue with Bultmann

TRANSLATED BY JOHN RICHES

FORTRESS PRESS Philadelphia

This book is a translation of 'Theologie und Verkündigung', published by J. C. B. Mohr (Paul Siebeck), Tübingen, in 1962.

Printed in Great Britain by
Northumberland Press Limited
Gateshead

To

FRIEDRICH GOGARTEN

Preface

The first three parts of this study are based on a lecture on *'Wissenschaftliche Theologie und kirchliche Verkündigung'* which was held on 19th April 1961 at the conference of contributors and subscribers to the *Göttinger Predigtmeditationen* in Arnoldshain (cf. MPTh/GPM 1961, 294*ff*, MPTh 50, 1961, 378*ff*); it was also given in various forms at Rickling/Schleswig-Holstein, Herrenalb, Tübingen, and Zürich. After it had been revised for printing it became too long for publication in a journal. Above all, so many additions had been made to the discussion with Bultmann in the third part that it had become the major part of the work. In order to point the way forward to further theological reflection, I also added theses on Christology and Ecclesiology which I had given at the end of lectures in the winter term 1960-61 and in the summer term 1961.

Thus the published work bears the marks of its origins. It would perhaps have been desirable to rewrite it in the form of a more extensive monograph. This however proved impracticable for I was principally concerned that the discussion which Bultmann had summarised in his Akademie essay 'The relation of the primitive Christian message of Christ to the historical Jesus', should be taken a stage further, and—and this seems to me most important of all in this discussion—that one should now at this time attempt to get to the root of the problem of the situation of proclamation. I certainly do not claim that my contribution to the discussion is anything like complete or definitive. But I hope that it will contribute to gaining clarity in theology and—above all—that it will throw light on the unity of the tasks of scientific theology and church proclamation which have again today been thrown into doubt.

I am afraid that the presentation of the work will not make it easy for the reader. On the one hand there are many long notes. As footnotes they threatened to submerge the text, and they have therefore been gathered at the back of the book. Not only my own comments but the many quotations in full are intended to make it easier to check the accuracy of what I have said and as aids to the reader's own study of the problem, since page references alone, even if they are looked up, are of little use if it is not possible to give a precise indication of the passage intended. On the other hand the reader will notice the lack of reasons for, and explanations of the theses in parts IV and V, and will probably be disconcerted by the compression of the rather demanding formulations in those sections. Indeed, not only here but in the whole book I should have said a great deal more in order to develop the matter more fully and to take the relevant literature into account. For this reason I would ask the reader to read what there is all the more carefully.

I take the opportunity of publicly congratulating Friedrich Gogarten on his 75th birthday by dedicating this book to him. I hope that he and his friend Rudolf Bultmann, to whom this reply to his essay is intended as a sign of esteem and thanks, will recognise and accept how much the following work is indebted to both of them.

Zürich, 1st December 1961

It has been decided to omit from the English edition Ebeling's final essay on Walter Künneth, 'Nachwort: Hinweis auf ein Pamphlet'. (Publishers.)

Contents

Abbreviations

AAG	Abhandlung der Akademie des Wissenschaft in Göttingen
AAH	Abhandlungen der Heidelberger Akademie der Wissenschaften, Phil.-hist. Kl.
AAMz	Abhandlungen der geistes- und sozialwissenschaftlichen Klasse der Akademie der Wissenschaften und der Literatur. Mainz
AKG	Arbeiten zur Kirchengeschichte
BFChTh	Beiträge zur Förderung christlicher Theologie
BHTh	Beiträge zur historischen Theologie
BSLK	*Die Bekenntnisschriften der evang.-luth. Kirche*, ed. Deutscher Evangelischer Kirchenausschuss, 1956^{3}
Clem	*Luthers Werke in Auswahl*, ed. O. Clemen, 1959^{5}
EaF	R. Bultmann, *Existence and Faith*, 1961 (= selections from GuV I and III)
EKL	*Evangelisches Kirchenlexikon*, 1955*ff*
EPaT	R. Buttmann, *Essays Philosophical and Theological*, 1955 (=GuV II)
EvTh	*Evangelische Theologie*
FSThR	*Forschungen zur systematischen Theologie und Religionsphilosophie*
FJK	O. Ritschl, *Festschrift für J. Kaftan*, 1920.
GPM	*Göttinger Predigtmeditationen* (included in MPTh)
GuV	R. Bultmann, *Glauben und Verstehen* I 1964^{2}; II 1952; III 1959 (=EaF and EPaT)
HZ	*Historische Zeitschrift*
KaM	*Kerygma and Myth*, ed. H. Bartsch (=KuM)
KD	K. Barth, *Die kirchliche Dogmatik*
KuD	*Kerygma und Dogma*

Abbreviations

KuM	*Kerygma und Mythos*, ed. H. W. Bartsch I 1948; II 1952 (= KaM)
MdKI	*Materialdienst des Konfessionskundlichen Instituts*
MPTh	*Monatsschrift für Pastoraltheologie*
NF	Neue Folge = New series
RAC	*Reallexikon für Antike und Christentum*, 1941*ff*
RE³	*Realencyklopädie für protestantische Theologie und Kirche*, 1896*ff*³
RGG²⁻³	*Die Religion in Geschichte und Gegenwart*, 1927*ff*²; 1957*ff*³
SAH	Sitzungsberichte der Heidelberger Akademie der Wissenschaften, Phil.-hist. Kl.
SgV	Sammlung gemeinverständlicher Vorträge und Schriften aus dem Gebiet der Theologie und Religionsgeschichte
TheolNT	R. Bultmann, *Theologie des Neuen Testaments*, 1953 = *Theology of the New Testament*, 1955
ThEx	*Theologische Existenz heute*
ThLZ	*Theologische Literaturzeitung*
ThR NF	*Theologische Rundschau*
ThSt	*Theologische Studien*
ThW	*Theologisches Wörterbuch zum Neuen Testament*, 1933*ff*
WA	M. Luther, *Werke. Kritische Gesamtausgabe* (Weimarer Ausgabe), 1883*ff*
WaF	G. Ebeling, *Word and Faith*, 1963 (= WuG)
WuG	G. Ebeling, *Wort und Glaube*, 1962² (= WaF)
ZNW	*Zeitschrift für die neutestamentliche Wissenschaft*
ZSTh	*Zeitschrift für systematische Theologie*
ZThK	*Zeitschrift für Theologie und Kirche*
ZW	*Zeitwende*

I

The tension between 'scientific theology' and 'church proclamation'

Our concern is proclamation. Now it may seem that proclamation and concern are ill-matched partners. An essential part of proclamation is certainty and from this should spring joy. We mean of course christian proclamation. For this, by its own claim, is the word which brings certainty. To be its servant is to spread joy. Yet this gives us cause to reflect whether the activities which lay claim to such a title may with justice be called proclamation, no matter how much energy is spent on their preparation. We shall however be well advised to avoid sweeping statements in this matter. We would hesitate to suggest that the difficulties which confront our age are greater than ever before; nor should one, particularly where proclamation is concerned, be taken in too easily by outward appearances. Nevertheless, the general impression is alarming. In large part the power of proclamation to bring certainty seems to have been lost. Most preachers seem to get along without it. Such powerful preaching as there is is more likely to draw its strength from the compulsion of the religious law than from the liberating urgency of the Gospel.

One of the symptoms which indicates that all is not well here is the frequent complaint one hears about the tension or gap between theology and proclamation. Now whatever the justice of such a charge, it does at least indicate that there is a real problem here. At the one extreme scientific theology is accused of having departed from the congregation of the faithful and of having destroyed the foundations of faith with its critical reason. At the other extreme one may indeed be gripped by the study of theology and the knowledge that it must lead to proclamation, and yet find the way to such proclamation barred because one is unable to reconcile the insights of theology with the traditional types of sermon and the expectations of the so-called 'faithful' congregation. Between these two extremes there lies a wide range of serious attempts to deal honestly with the tension between scientific theology and church proclamation, attempts to avoid pursuing the one without regard for the other, attempts above all constantly to find a new way through from exegesis to the sermon. On the other hand there is a whole circus full of the different personifications of folly: the stubbornness of those who persist in their imagined faith or knowledge; the shifting equivocation of those who attempt to do justice to all sides but never dare to face the contradictions in which they involve themselves; there are the theological jugglers who play with concepts and jargon without ever really getting to the heart of the matter; there are those furiously taken up (or should one say tied up?) in the business of jumping through the hoop of one sermon to reach the next, complaining bitterly the while, but secretly by no means dissatisfied to be free of the business of theological reflection.

Yet we must resist the temptation of filling in the details and colours of this very rough sketch, and instead move straight to the heart of the matter: for we wish to further the cause of proclamation, and that means that our concern is with those who—whether they know it or not—wait on our proclamation. So we shall delay as little as possible over preliminaries, not because as theologians our time is short,[1] but because the time is necessarily always propitious for treating of the subject matter of theology, if it does indeed treat of God and not of mere nothing.

Proclamation is always beset with trials and threatened with misunderstanding, even in ages where it apparently meets fewest obstacles for its understanding. Yet in certain respects preaching has become more difficult today because the situation in which christian proclamation has to make itself understood has become more problematical.[2] To reduce what is in fact a highly complicated and comprehensive revolution in man's thought to a formula which is perhaps all too simple (which may however be not unfruitful for reflection), the traditional metaphysical understanding of reality is being replaced by the historical understanding of reality.[3] Now I have put this in the present tense because although this process started some centuries ago, it is not yet fully accomplished and has produced many hybrids; at the same time men are far from agreeing on its interpretation. All the difficulties which face proclamation today have in some way to do with the transition to a radically historical way of thought. Now this is intended as a statement about the roots of this transition, and as such makes no claim to describe its (more superficial) manifestations. Yet even these seem to indicate that a new factor has come into play at a very deep level which now leaves men with only the most tenuous relationship to traditional christian language.

Yet lest we should fall under the spell of mere catch-phrases, let us try and describe some of the traits of this historicality which so dominates modern man in all spheres of his activity and which takes the most diverse forms, including even—paradoxically enough—complete oblivion of history, and the improvidence of those who live only for the present moment. It will be best to start with the relationship to history which is still afforded by tradition. This is the simple process of *traditio*,[4] which is a distinctive element in the lives of men together, both between men and their contemporaries and between succeeding generations. Without *traditio* there would be no spirit, no real humanity. *Traditio* is conveyed in the main by the obvious and self-explanatory ways of speech, custom, human ordinances, by the preservation and propagation of cultural values. The formation of this *traditio* is of vital importance, and is consciously furthered by the different means of preserving, propagating and commemorating historical reality. Even in modern times men are largely dependent on this relation to history.

Now what is new about this is the remarkable way in which interest in the past has been intensified. It is not merely that people have come to take more interest in the past; rather this interest seems to threaten the old way of living within an accepted *traditio*. The critical interest in the past aims to free men from its oppressive domination. Instead of passively allowing the past to make its presence felt in the normal way, men have now become active and attempt to wrest secrets from it which it is not always eager to yield. The authority of the past has been replaced by the critical examination of the prevailing views of history, of our 'heritage', of prejudices, legends, and even of the lies of history. The emphasis has shifted from tradition to research. Man need no longer feel that he has his place within a very few strands of tradition, but may now seek out historical encounters for himself at will. It is still of course true that man's relation to his own particular historical circumstances may best be characterised as *'Geworfenheit'*.* Yet just as one can rise above particular traditions and can shake oneself free of them (even if this means forfeiting one's sheltered existence and being drawn into the ranks of the spiritual refugees), one is also able, thanks to the breadth of modern historical learning, to take refuge in other ages, to choose out for oneself another

* Literally 'thrownness'. Heidegger uses the term to describe the phenomenon that man finds himself in a situation that is not of his own choosing, that at birth he is thrown haphazard into life, into the environment which plays such a large part in his formation. (Translator's note.)

home, and so to question even more radically one's own sense of belonging to the present age.

This brings us to the most important point of all. It was Troeltsch who said that the expression 'purely historical' (*rein historisch*) presupposed a complete world-view of its own. What is decisive is not the development of increasingly refined methods of historical enquiry, but the radical historicisation (*Historisierung*) of man himself, of his ways of thought, and of reality as a whole. We can now only understand something as historically conditioned, as a part of an historical development. On the one hand only the historical has any validity; on the other all real validity has been taken away from the historical. The consequences of this may manifest themselves in very different ways. There is firstly historicism. The present is lost from sight under the painstaking labour of amassing detailed facts about the past. The future withers away, choked by the enormous growth of the historical consciousness. One no longer dares to exist in one's own right; one is content to borrow one's style from the past. Yet by mastering all the historical styles one only succeeds in losing all style oneself. However, this is less characteristic of our age than what one might call the activist view of history. Here we find the prototype in the emancipated, revolutionary man. He strives to master the world by technological means; he is rootless, reduced to the state of a mere functionary of his own needs or of the totalitarian machine. As such he has only the most tenuous and arbitrary relationship to past history as he concentrates his efforts towards the mastery of future history. There is yet a third attitude to history, which till now has been little noticed, and this I would like to call the 'diaconal'[5] view. On such a view the radical meaning of history is to be grasped as modern secular man listens and responds to the past in an attitude both of submission and of readiness to set to rights that which has gone before.

Christian faith, which seems to be wedded to an authoritarian view of tradition, has felt the force of this new historical understanding of reality at one point in particular. For the crumbling fortifications of the orthodox doctrine of Scripture were unable to withstand the onslaught of the critical-historical method.[6] While the church taught the verbal inspiration of the scriptures through God, historical enquiry was showing the Bible to be the result of a long and complicated development which could be charted by the various disciplines of tradition-history, form criticism, literary criticism, and by an examination of the history of the canon and the texts. Its various sources and historical strata were isolated. Many of the details about the history of the documents, as for example their authorship, have been shown to be no more than pious inventions. Much which was before considered historical is now recognised as legendary. Parallels from other religions have shown that the portrayal of the divine acts of revelation is mythical in character. The biblical view of the universe of time and space emerges as very different from our own.

The theology of the last two hundred years was itself responsible for this inventory. At the same time it has attempted, however tentatively, to show that this in no way alters the foundations of our faith. On the contrary, in many ways the Bible becomes more plastic; it begins to speak with new force; one's attention is drawn to the essentials of the faith; the use of the critical-historical method is a guard against an understanding of revelation which is contrary to the spirit of the reformation.[7] The remarkable thing is that while in general the church has a very uneasy conscience about the whole matter, it still tends to leave things shamefully obscure which are glaringly obvious to anyone with any insight. The result is that the rift between theology and the so-called 'faith of the congregation' has become oppressively wide. And absurdly enough theology is held responsible for these problems. The traditional faith of the congregation sets itself up as the yard-stick of orthodoxy. The resultant anxiety and underlying insincerity show that faith has been disastrously changed into the work of appropriating the incredible.[8]

Only the most desperate apologetics could gain even a hearing for such 'faith' from modern man with his fundamentally confused historical understanding of reality. Yet it fails to realise its true obligation of presenting this man, whom it regards as an enemy whom it is incapable of loving, with the testimony which would bring him the gift of certainty. Church proclamation of this sort is *de facto* propaganda against the church.[9]

Yet we must make no mistake about the nature of the difficulties which have led to this state of affairs. It is expecting a very great deal from people who have no theological education to ask them to assimilate the results of a critical historical exposition of the scriptures. The tension between a naïve understanding of text and its proper interpretation is in danger of becoming so great that the ordinary member of a congregation can make very little of it. What is really needed is that we should find a way of witnessing to the christian faith which is so convincingly simple and radical as to overcome problems raised by the tension between the letter and the spirit, or at least to show clearly that they are secondary problems. Yet it is clear that we will only find such a way of witnessing to the christian faith if the questions which are inevitably raised by historical enquiry are not forced underground where they can only do very great damage. This means that one cannot avoid these difficulties by attempting to secure an area for faith where it is free from attack,[10] on the principle that faith should never become dependent on the vicissitudes of historical enquiry. Rather the very historicity of faith demands a proclamation which is prepared to run the gauntlet of history. This in turn raises problems which are much wider than the mere correction of details in the tradition which historical criticism shows to be faulty. The necessity of embracing a radically historical mode of thought has put an end to all supranaturalism and means that the traditional language of the church[11] has become powerless, to such an extent that it is only in the sphere of historical thought that the problem of the language of faith really becomes crucial. For how can talk about God have any meaning if only the historical is real?[12] This points to a reconstruction of christian thought, the extent and direction of which we can at the moment only guess at. It is not hard then to understand the atmosphere of anxiety in the church, if at this point theology itself is still fumbling in the dark.

We have tried to show that the tension between theology and proclamation about which we have heard so many complaints is the consequence of the changed situation in which we preach, and that moreover it is a consequence which we should not merely accept with resignation. To be more precise, it is the consequence on the one hand of the preacher's unwillingness to take seriously the new situation in which he has to preach, and on the other of the fact that although theology has taken seriously the problems raised by modern historical thought, it has as yet failed to deal with them in a manner which is really adequate, convincing and helpful. Clearly the ways in which people normally discuss this tension are sheerly absurd. It is not enough to make the charge that it is theology which is the cause of all our difficulties—while in fact they spring from the situation in which we have to preach. Nor will we get very far with the notion that we can get round all the problems by simply denying them. Yet the fundamental misconception lies in the idea that we are dealing with two independent authorities which can each accuse the other of failing in its duty.

If we think of theology as responsible reflection on proclamation, then clearly we cannot think of it in separation from proclamation. Theology without proclamation is empty, proclamation without theology is blind. It is of course quite proper to attempt to map out the differences between the two. Theology constitutes a science, proclamation constitutes the church. Both definitions need more precise formulation in certain respects. Can we really claim that theology is a science and if so in what sense?[13] What is it in concrete terms which characterises proclamation as constitutive of the church?[14] And just as proclamation, properly speaking, is *eo ipso* church proclamation—as that which makes the church the church and as that in which the church is seen to be the church—so one must also see that the phrase 'scientific theology' is a tautology, that is, if one is not to narrow down the concept of science so far as to make it unusable. There is no choice between scientific and unscientific theology. If the proper task of theology is responsible reflection on the event of proclamation, then we may clearly not interpret the fact that they have different places on the map, in such a way that we lose the unity of subject matter between theology and proclamation. They are different ways of speaking responsibly about God.[15] So we shall meet our basic problem in the sphere of theology, because it is the problem of proclamation. We will encounter it first in the form of the duality of historical and dogmatic theology which has arisen in modern times. We shall now proceed to a discussion of the problem at this level.

II

Historical and dogmatic theology

The change in the understanding of reality and the consciousness of truth in modern times has served to bring out into the open the tension between academic theology and ordinary lay Christianity, which till then had largely gone unnoticed. Equally it was at this time (and this perhaps gives an indication of its cause) that there occurred the division of theology into historical and dogmatic disciplines, a division which made all previous ones seem comparatively unimportant.

Now if the task of the theologian is to reflect on the event of proclamation as one who shares responsibility for it, this means that one's reflections will be directed both towards proclamation which has already taken place and towards proclamation which is to take place in future.[1] Theology stands or falls by the indivisibility of these two dimensions; the actual occurrence of proclamation has its reference to proclamation that has already occurred, while the occurrence of proclamation charges and authorises one to further proclamation. This might lead one to say that the phrase 'historical theology' is a tautology. For the task which theology is given to do is identical with the gift it receives from tradition, with that which theology and theology alone has to say, and with that which gives it its urgency. The task of handing on this tradition, which claims absolute truth and healing power for itself, the task of reporting what has happened and proclaiming it as normative is clearly constitutive for theology. Thus it might seem that such *historein* was also in fact *homologein* and *eo ipso* belonged to dogmatic theology.

Modern historical thought has made the previously self-evident unity of historical and dogmatic speech so problematic that one might have been tempted to despair of the unity of theology: indeed, to doubt its very possibility. If theology's reference to history and tradition was to appear as more than a mere pretence, then obviously theology had to take account of the modern understanding of historical studies. This in itself—regardless of any particular criticisms which such studies might bring to light—meant that theology was split in two.

For the sake of proclamation, theology cannot be content with mere statements of historical fact, but must go on to make dogmatic statements. It is only in the sphere of dogmatics, properly understood, that theology bears fruit. While the historical disciplines tend to deal with particular questions, dogmatics deals with the whole. Historical disciplines say 'Thus it was!' Dogmatic theology says: 'Thus it is!' It is not concerned merely with historical accuracy, however much it may be dependent on it. For such accuracy does not complete the task of dogmatic theology. It is concerned with the truth in which the future reveals itself. The historical disciplines permit us to keep a certain distance between ourselves and our subject matter—indeed, they insist in some ways that we should do so. This does not of course simply mean that we have to be mere disinterested spectators. There is also a certain type of engagement and even loyalty which has its place in historical work. Yet Ranke's ideal of the exclusion of the self very often means that the self is included in the strongest possible way.[2] Nevertheless there is a fundamental difference between this and dogmatic theology. In the latter it is *eo ipso* impossible to exclude oneself from the subject, for if it merely gives an account of the history of dogmatics, it ceases to be dogmatic theology and becomes historical theology. In dogmatic theology the theologian identifies himself with the subject matter of theology. For he can only speak of this in the form of assertions, affirmatively.[3] He allows himself to be engrossed by it, he takes responsibility for it. Thus the utterance of the dogmatic theologian is like that of the preacher. The preacher is by definition a witness. A dogmatic theologian, no matter how learned he may be, is of no use unless he is certain of what he is saying. As such, dogmatic theology brings out very well the relation of theology to speech about God. One cannot speak about God in a disinterested, objective and neutral way. If one does, then in effect one is no longer speaking about God. Speech about God cannot occur except in a context in which the only proper use of language is in the form of a (dogmatic) confession of faith. In this way the phrase 'dogmatic theology' is also, properly speaking, a tautology. Theology ceases to be theology if it is no longer concerned to bring God to expression, and so to make the claim to speak the truth in the sense of the simply necessary. Contrasted with this, historical theology, in the strict sense of the word, would be a *contradictio in adiecto*, for one cannot speak of God historically, at least not if by 'historically' one means an objectified view of the past.

However, the historical nature of theology's subject matter has meant that it has not been able to ignore historical thought. Thus one would give a completely false picture of the matter if one suggested that dogmatic theology remained unaltered while the new historical disciplines were being established as competitors, critics, or merely as complementary to the older science. For the real upheaval took place within dogmatic theology itself. Once historical theology was accepted, it was impossible for dogmatic theology to remain unchanged. It had to take a share in the responsibility for historical theology and could be taken seriously as dogmatic theology only if it was prepared to enter into the historical work of modern times. Indeed the theological character of so-called historical theology was dependent on the success of these reconsiderations on the part of dogmatic theology. If theology allowed itself to be reduced to mere 'Historie' in the modern sense, then it would become no more than a branch of the history of religions.

In such a situation the theological character of historical theology will only come to the fore if the historian becomes conscious of his dogmatic task; this can only happen when he becomes aware that the normal self-understanding of historical study in modern times is inadequate and illogical, simply because it does not do justice to the true nature of the historical. Dogmatic theology is not constituted by breaking free from the strait bonds of historical study; it comes into being as one reflects on the nature of this study, and that means getting to the root of the real question of history. This is the aim of the questions raised in hermeneutics. It is only by travelling the road of hermeneutics that historical and dogmatic theology will be able to come together again. This is the only way of keeping open the possibility of doing theology today. Theologians have realised that instead of the two disciplines merely ignoring one another or senselessly struggling for precedence, they should be seen as two aspects of the same hermeneutic task of theology, which can only be separated from one another at the cost of their own integrity. One must be a dogmatic theologian for the sake of historical theology and one must be an historical theologian for the sake of dogmatic theology.

We can show why it is necessary to have two different disciplines to carry out the same task by reference to the distinction in the meaning of *traditio* between *traditum* and *actus tradendi*. Historical theology is primarily concerned with the *traditum* as such, with the fact that it was handed down, and the question of what, and how it was handed down. So historical theology concentrates on textually and chronologically different complexes of tradition, on different *tradita*. The historian is primarily interested in historical data as data. By contrast the task of dogmatic theology is primarily to observe[4] the *traditio*. Of course this means that it must look at the *traditum*, at the diversity of the theologically relevant texts. Yet the specific task of dogmatics is not to examine these texts simply to see what it is that has been handed down, but itself to participate in the *actus tradendi*.

This again points to the extraordinary proximity of dogmatic theology to the event of proclamation. It is not our intention to overlook the distinction between dogmatic theology and proclamation. Dogmatic theology is concerned to reflect critically on the proclamation for which it is responsible, and such reflection will necessarily be of a general character. Proclamation on the other hand is the *actus tradendi* in its most concrete form. However this distinction will necessarily fade into the background as soon as we start to define the difference between historical and dogmatic theology. It would be a fundamental mistake to confuse the historical task of examining the *traditum* or *tradita* with the *actus tradendi* itself, or alternatively to confuse the *actus tradendi* with the mere retailing of historical *tradita*. In spite of the very close connection which exists between the two, there is the greatest difference between on the one hand examining the *traditum* as *traditum*, and on the other, not allowing the *traditum* to rest as *traditum* but oneself handing it on as *tradendum*. The full significance of this cannot be grasped as long as one thinks of the *tradendum* as a traditional text. Christian proclamation is concerned with the 'event' of a tradition, which is the tradition of an 'event'; it is not merely the tradition of an event that is past, but—although the two by no means exclude each other—is the tradition of a present and continuous event.

This in turn explains the different subject matter of historical and dogmatic theology. The subject matter of historical theology—as determined by the 'tradition-event'—is the numerous theologically relevant texts, in which the tradition has been recorded as an historical *traditum*. On the other hand it would be a mistake to think that one can indicate the subject matter of dogmatic theology by pointing to any particular text, whether it be the Holy Scriptures—in which case dogmatics would obviously be in competition with the historical disciplines—or to any group of texts peculiar to dogmatics, as for example the traditional church dogmas,[5] whose examination is more properly ascribed to the history of doctrine or to symbolics.

There are two main tendencies in theology which misconstrue the task of dogmatics in a traditionalistic way (though neither tendency is ever in fact carried to its logical conclusion): dogmatism and biblicism. Taken to its extreme, either of these relieves the theologian of his real responsibility. Carried out to its logical conclusion it would mean that theology would finish its career as a form of positivism. Now positivist theology is not bad theology because it holds fast to that which is given, to the tradition. If it really did that, then everything would be all right. It is no alternative to this to offer a theology decked out in the colours of progressive thought which sets light to tradition. This is more likely to lead to intellectual prostitution than to sound theology, and good taste alone should make us despise it. I hope these remarks will be sufficient to prevent at source any misconstruction of my theological aims. It is not the insistence on the given, on tradition, which is the objection against a theology which has become traditionalistic and positivistic. For although such theology appears to hold fast to the tradition, it in fact abandons it. For it 'presents' it simply as *traditum*, and that is to say simply as a preterite. It fails to answer for it in the present word-event which directs men to the future, in which the *traditum* is fulfilled in the *traditio*. The *traditum* can only fulfil the purpose for which it was handed down if it is taken up into the *actus tradendi*, i.e. if the written text is transformed into the 'event of the Spirit' of the spoken word.

The thesis that the subject matter of dogmatic theology is not simply a particular text or texts, is not intended to detract from the importance of the texts but rather to bring out their real value. Dogmatic theology fulfils its task of exposition, not by employing methods which cut across historical exegesis, but by making the change from an historical to a dogmatic 'relation of understanding'[6] which the subject itself demands. In dealing with a text there is a transition from an exposition *of* the text to an exposition *by* the text (i.e. that one is concerned to be taught the truth about oneself by the text). There is a corresponding transition in the meaning of the phrase 'exposition of the text', from an objective genitive to a subjective genitive. It is no longer the text which is to be expounded and which needs expounding; now we see that the purpose of the text is itself to expound and illumine and create. For the text is not there for its own sake, but for the sake of the word-event which is the origin and also the future of the text. Word-event is the exposition-event which is carried out by the Word. For this reason the text exists for the benefit of the exposition-event which is the origin and future of the text. For the Word which once happened and which has been recorded in the form of a text as an event which has occurred, must with the help of the text again become Word, and so come into being as the expounding Word. We may call that which happens in the word-event exposition, because it is the nature of the Word to illumine that which is dark, to bring light into darkness. As such, if it is the Word which concerns all men, it is able to show men the truth of what they really are. One can only grasp the true depth of such an exposition-event, when one has seen that it brings men to the truth in such a way that at the same time it both reveals and transforms reality.

The subject-matter of dogmatic theology is therefore the word-event itself, in which the reality of man is shown in its true light. Now the phrase 'the reality of man' should not be taken here to mean mere 'anthropology'.[7] What is meant is the reality which confronts man and which constitutes his humanity in all its diversity; we do not mean the abstracted reality of man which is separated from all other reality, but rather the reality of man which, surrounded by and exposed to all other reality, can only so be properly called reality. The word-event in which the reality of man is shown in its true light is the word-event which makes man true and so for the first time real. And so now we can say that the subject of dogmatic theology is the event, which occurs only in the Word, of the coming of God to man. Using a phrase of Luther's to bring out the character of this word-event unambiguously, we could say: the subject of dogmatic theology, the *subjectum theologiae* is *homo peccator* and *deus justificans*.[8] It would be better to replace the term 'subject' by the word 'cause' (*Sache*) which has its etymological origins in the law-suit and as such is more suited to the word-event; thus it means that for which the Word conducts a suit.[9] So we can reformulate: the cause of dogmatic theology is the *deus justificans hominem peccatorem*.

Now if theology is to conduct this suit, it must obviously direct its attention to certain texts; on the one hand to an infinite number of texts, i.e. to all those texts which are in any way relevant, either for or against, to the case; and on the other hand to the Holy Scriptures with their special position within the canon. This contrast between the many and the one brings out the fact that the Bible can only perform the special service which dogmatic theology expects from it, if it is not isolated from the voices which interpret and contradict it. One must not attempt to silence artificially the other texts which stand alongside the Bible; rather one must first see how the Bible measures up to them, whether it will put them to silence or whether it may not in fact allow their voices to be properly heard for the first time. If we are to do justice to the peculiar dignity of the Holy Scriptures, then all the other texts which concern dogmatic theology must, at least potentially, be present and assembled around the scriptures. Otherwise it is impossible to do justice to the principle of *sola scriptura*. Yet the 'cause' of dogmatic theology is not this text or this collection of texts, but it is the word-event made possible by this text among the collection of texts; for they enable us to answer for the word-event which is the origin and future of the biblical text, to take part in its coming to pass. The task of dogmatic theology is to *advocate* the cause of theology.

Now it is possible to give some account of the cause of theology in short formulae: faith, Jesus Christ, the Gospel, the Word of God, or the most simple and most difficult of all—God. But this is not to advocate the cause of theology. This only happens when it is set forward, i.e. when it is set in relation to the reality which confronts men, when it is spoken to him. The cause of dogmatic theology and the reality which confronts men are not two separate items; one cannot deal with one first and then relate it to the other afterwards, as for example one might ascertain the cause of dogmatic theology by historical means and then in a separate process might go on to apply it to the present. Of course it is of great importance that one should make sure of the accuracy of the tradition by historical means. But it is one thing to advocate the cause of theology historically and thus to remain in its debt, and quite another to espouse the cause of dogmatic theology in such a way that the cause of theology itself is advocated.

Of course the distinction between historical and dogmatic speech in theology is necessarily rather abstract. If the work is done properly then the two run inseparably into one another. It is impossible to do historical work on theology without becoming involved in dogmatics, and vice versa, even if it is relatively true to say that in one case we are chiefly interested in the texts, in which reality is expressed and addressed, while in the other case it is primarily the reality itself with which we are occupied, which is expressed and addressed by the Word of theology. If on the one hand dogmatic theology is not a mere historical representation of the *traditum* as such, but the observation of the cause of theology in the *actus tradendi*; and if on the other hand dogmatic theology is not primarily concerned with the texts as witness to the Word which came to pass, but with the word-event itself, then we can see the real breadth of the task of hermeneutics. For the sake of the texts, and this does not simply mean for the sake of preserving them, but in order to put them into effect,[10] to carry them out, dogmatic theology is directed to reality; and for the sake of reality (and this means speaking to it in such a way that one corrects it and shows it in its true light), dogmatic theology is directed to texts which have been handed down. It does not recite words that have already been spoken, but brings God's Word to expression. It is the language school of proclamation.[11]

III

Kerygma and the historical Jesus

We still however have to consider the problem of proclaiming the Gospel today in the acutest form in which it is raised for theology.

1. The problem of Christology

In spite of the richness of thematic material on which the christian preacher may draw, christian preaching may nevertheless be precisely characterised as the proclamation of Christ. The kerygma is *eo ipso* kerygma of Christ. When we think over the problem of proclamation today, our attention inevitably focuses on the problem of Christology. How can we hold ourselves accountable for the basic christological claims which we make in our preaching today? Is there perhaps any connection between the inability of our christian proclamation to bring certainty to its hearers (which we noticed above) and the questions which are raised when we consider the relation of proclamation to Christology? This is not just one particular issue in the problem of proclamation; rather it is in the nature of the matter that the problem of proclamation and the problem of Christology should fuse into one. For 'homology', speaking boldly, with certainty, is the primary form of speech which we use when speaking of Christ, just because we confess Jesus Christ as God's Word; that is, as the Word which brings certainty, which gives us power to take up the language of faith.[1]

The emphasis on historical thought in modern times has raised the gravest problems for theology precisely in the field of Christology. But it is not enough to give a general explanation of the crisis which has been occasioned in the christian faith by the onslaught of the modern age, by saying that this must naturally show itself most clearly in the central definition of that faith, as faith in Jesus Christ. The matter can be more precisely stated thus: the relation of faith and history which is constitutive for the christian faith finds its decisive form in Christology. For this reason the conflict with the historical thought of modern times must be decided in the field of Christology. The success of Christology depends on one thing: whether we can show convincingly that in Jesus God has 'come to expression', in such a way that faith must constantly return to its roots in Jesus. The fact that the Christian stands simultaneously in a relationship to a particular historical phenomenon and to God is exemplified in the basic structure of the christological confession: *vere Deus—vere homo*. It is this that to unbelief has ever been the offence and foolishness of Christianity. Yet it is only in modern times that this has been radically questioned with regard to the understanding of reality which it implies.

In the first place, difficulties are raised for Christology by the examination of the biblical and dogmatic traditions by the methods of historical criticism. In Fr. Strauss' telling phrase: 'The real criticism of dogma is its own history.'[2] But over and above all the specific results of critical study, it is the understanding of historical reality itself, on which Christology rests, which threatens to prove fatal. The following list, while by no means complete, or for that matter in chronological order, must suffice to give some indication of this.

The first discovery was the difference between the preaching of Jesus and the early christian preaching of Christ, between the faith of Jesus himself and faith in him; and so alongside traditional Christology arose the modern quest for the historical Jesus. In the first place this was intended as an attack on old views; it was hoped that by returning to the historical Jesus one could free oneself from the Christ of dogmatics, that is to say from Christology. But there were others who hoped to provide an apologetic for Christology on the basis of the historical Jesus[3]—witness, for example, the importance attached to the question of the messianic consciousness of Jesus. We will deal below, briefly, with the much discussed failure of the quest for the historical Jesus.[4] For the moment it must suffice to give a warning against taking the short-sighted view that one can make christological capital out of this, that one is lucky to be freed from the dangers of historical enquiry by its own apparent suicide. The problem of the difference between the historical Jesus and the kerygmatic Christ remains, in spite of the fate of the enquiry into the life of Jesus.

A further discovery was that early christian Christology had found expression in many different forms, which by no means lent themselves to ready harmonisation. The very nature of the language used in these statements made it impossible to consider them as statements of objective historical fact. This was seen to be true both of the messianic titles and the kerygmatic formulae, as well as of the confessions of faith in narrative form. The study of the development of the tradition revealed many cases where it had been enriched by fictitious material and the formation of legends; but further one had to concede the presence of a great deal of mythological material, at least, that is if one follows modern historical thought in applying the concept of mythology to all supranatural elements in historical statements.[5] In this way Christology appears as no more than a later mythologising of the person of Jesus, which it is no longer possible for us to accept. However, neither is it possible for us to recover that which lay behind the process of mythologising. Thus, for example, Fr. Strauss, who was no great lover of traditional Christology, put it: 'The price of a man's deification is the irrevocable loss of his humanity.'[6]

Next we must notice a fundamental change in the problems which beset Christology. If Jesus is shown to be an historical person, then there can be no doubts in our minds about the reality of his humanity. To prove his historical existence is *eo ipso* to prove his humanity. There is, for us, no longer any danger of docetism,[7] whilst orthodox Christology, however much some may protest, cannot easily be cleared from such a charge.[8] Whereas traditional Christology assumed the fundamental truth of the *vere deus*, thus jeopardising the confession of faith in the *vere homo*, it is now the *vere deus* which raises the most acute problems for Christology.[9]

For the time is past—and this, however unwilling one is to recognise it, probably marks the most fundamental change in the question of Christology—when traditional Christology could as a matter of course take God, or more precisely the second Person of the Godhead, as an already known quantity about which it could then proceed to make christological statements in the narrow sense of the word.[10] Yet it is not only that belief in the Person of the Son of God, as a necessary condition of the understanding of Christology is denied to modern man, and with it the possibility of an approach to the understanding of Christology; it is also that the gradual disappearance of any form of world-view,[11] which allows for some sort of general belief in God, seems to have undermined the whole structure of Christology. Is there any sense—even if it were possible—in bringing man first to a belief in God, as a condition of bringing him to belief in Jesus Christ? Would not this imply that Jesus did not come to the ungodly after all?

Bultmann employed the concept of the kerygma in an attempt to come to grips with the problem of a Christology faced with radically new difficulties in making itself intelligible to the modern world. He used it to bring out the way in which the christian faith is directed simultaneously to history and to God. This rooting of Christology in the proclamation of the saving act of God in Jesus Christ shows how thoroughly orthodox in intention[12] is the whole of Bultmann's theological work. Instead of interpreting the mythological elements in terms of general truths, or even more or less hesitantly eliminating them altogether, he interpreted the mythological characteristics of Christology in terms of the kerygma which comes to expression in them, and thus retained the decisive relationship to history.[13] In Bultmann's view the existential interpretation which is required by his programme of demythologising in no way leads to the mere discussion and examination of the general possibilities of understanding one's existence, as those who would wrongly accuse his theology of reducing the Gospel to mere anthropology[14] suggest. Existential interpretation is much rather intended to bring out the theological significance of the mythological language of the New Testament, by interpreting it in such a way that the action of God in Christ and therefore the Person of Christ is stressed as the decisive saving event.

2. *The kerygma*

We must now examine at length the concept of the kerygma which has played such an important role in the enquiry into our proclamation today. Understood as the proclamation of the saving act of God in Christ, i.e. as christologically oriented proclamation, it has become part of the current coinage of present discussion.[1] In this however it has generally been divorced from Bultmann's hermeneutic considerations. Thus instead of providing a useful tool for hermeneutics, it has been erected into a formidable summary of everything which has to be proclaimed, and now threatens to conceal the real problems facing proclamation under a welter of high-sounding christological terminology. So it may be well to ask whether Bultmann himself has not neglected certain aspects of the problem of the kerygma. Has he really brought out with equal emphasis the relation to history and the relation to God?

If we inquire into the relation of the kerygma to history, we learn that Jesus' relevance for the kerygma is confined to the mere 'That' of his person,[2] to the mere fact *that* he existed. By strictly denying the relevance for the christian faith of the questions *What?* and *How?* in relation to the historical Jesus, Bultmann is not however attempting to make allowance in dogmatics for the unhappy state of the quest for the historical Jesus. The kerygmatic character of the sources can in itself neither forbid, nor indeed deny all prospects of success to, historical enquiry.[3] The so-called quest for the historical Jesus failed only in as far as it was governed by a particular idea of history, modelled on biographical development and psychological probability,[4] and further by rather superficial ideas about how one man can exert religious influence over another. Bultmann's position in regard to the historical Jesus is determined by theological considerations based on his concept of the kerygma, according to which, speech about God's saving act can only find its proper place within the relation of Word and faith. So any attempt to 'search behind' the kerygma for its legitimation, for a proof of its truth, is rejected with the utmost severity as being against the nature both of the kerygma and of faith.[5] Thus in Bultmann's interpretation the Word is, in the first place, characterised as the authority[6] which demands decision, and faith as obedient acceptance.[7] Any attempt to give grounds for the kerygma by demonstrating its origins in the historical Jesus, would, for Bultmann, be to break out of the relationship between Word and faith and so to lose sight of the kerygma. The paradoxical possibility of describing historical events as the eschatological action of God depends on the impossibility of portraying the mere That.[8] 'It is precisely because it cannot be proved that christian proclamation can ensure itself against the objection that it is nothing but mythology.'[9]

Now of course we would agree completely with Bultmann's resolution to confine speech about God's action strictly within the relationship between Word and faith; again, we would agree with his determination to preserve the purity of faith by rejecting all so-called proofs of faith, which can in the end only serve to destroy faith.[10] Yet the real question is whether Bultmann has seen far enough into this relationship between Word and faith. If one asks how the kerygma is to be understood, Bultmann replies—however much he may stress the character of the Word as authority and of faith as obedience—not, as one might expect, by demanding a *sacrificium intellectus*, but by pointing to the new self-understanding which is opened up by the kerygma.[11] Yet the kerygma, however much it may speak to and cast light on man's existence, is not merely speech about man's existence. It is also a testimony to that which has happened,[12] and as such it points us to a way of understanding these events. Of course the 'word-event' must not be divided into the imparting of historical information on the one hand, and address and challenge on the other; or, to put it another way, into an understanding related firstly to a past tense and secondly to a future. Yet how are the two sides which we have distinguished related to each other?

If the kerygma is the proclamation of the fact of Jesus Christ, i.e. of his coming, death and resurrection as the eschatological saving event, then we can formulate the question about understanding the kerygma as follows: What has the understanding of such kerygmatic statements to do with the self-understanding suggested by the kerygma itself? Why must the Word which comes to fruition in the 'faith-event' be *the* Word which comes expressly from the 'Christ-event'? Why is the self-understanding of faith dependent on kerygmatic statements relating to historical events? What do these events which the kerygma brings to expression, contribute to the understanding of the kerygma as kerygma, i.e. to the understanding of that which is intended by the kerygma? What of the intelligibility of the kerygma when one can no longer make sense of such fundamental components of the kerygma as 'God's action', even of 'God'? What becomes of Bultmann's attempt to found a theology on the concept of the kerygma, if language about God, his action and his eschatological deed, which (as in traditional Christology) is taken for granted, is no longer meaningful or intelligible?[13] On Bultmann's own view Jesus Christ cannot help him at this point. For here the questions *what* he was and *how* he was become irrelevant when one turns to the decisive fact *that* God has acted in him.[14] How then can one avoid the impression, if the evaluation of Jesus in the kerygma remains unintelligible, that we are dealing with no more than an abstract mythologumenon? How does the basis of such kerygmatic statements, and with it the basis of faith, come to expression?

Bultmann does not inquire after the basis of faith, because he sees the question as fundamentally opposed to the nature of faith.[15] Now this would indeed be so, if the question really expected an answer which would no longer allow faith to seek its credentials in the Word alone, and which would thus sully the purity of faith. But the question of the basis of faith must never be seen as an attempt to establish faith on a foundation foreign to its nature, which would thus render faith itself partly or wholly superfluous.[16] It is rather the question what makes faith faith, whence stems faith, what gives faith its freedom, and what it is that enables faith to remain pure.[17] Both in the understanding of the Bible and of the Reformers this is nothing other than the Word of God. Thus the basis of faith would be the Word of God. But what does this mean? Could we substitute 'kerygma' for it? Then indeed the kerygma would set a definitive limit on our inquiry into the basis of faith. For the question of the basis of the Word of God would obviously be meaningless, in so far as it expected an answer in terms of anything outside that which we encountered in the Word and the Word alone, namely God. Is then the question of the basis of the kerygma really meaningless? Bultmann, in spite of his constant denunciation of the question, seems unable to avoid formulations which speak of authorisation in respect of the kerygma.[18] But how are the kerygma and the Word of God related to one another? What is really meant by kerygma?

It would seem quite easy to give Bultmann's answer to the question. In most cases at any rate he understands it to mean the proclamation of Christ which arose after the death of Jesus. This was the message of the eschatological saving act of God in Jesus Christ, a message which brought the church into being. This proclamation has been ceaselessly renewed and handed down; it has not of course been restricted to any particular formula, but has been handed down as christian preachers have struggled to preserve the identical christological meaning of the kerygmatic formulation.[19] However, the nature of Bultmann's position is such that this apparently simple answer demands certain modifications. On occasions he calls Jesus' proclamation 'kerygma'.[20] In the light of his predominant use of the term, this could easily be explained as a broad and improper use of the word which must therefore as far as possible be avoided in favour of a more narrow use of the concept.[21] Now there is here something quite fundamental at stake. What 'structural moments' serve to make the wider use of the term possible, while at the same time it is only the narrow use which is correct?

The form of the word *kērygma* permits two interpretations: that which is called out (the content of the proclamation) and the calling out (the act of proclamation). Both uses occur in the New Testament, although the second is overwhelmingly the more common.[22] In discussion of the concept of kerygma the case has often been made for a sharp distinction between the formal and the material sense,[23] and often indeed for limiting the use of the word entirely to the formal meaning.[24] I have no wish at the moment to open again the question of the New Testament use of the word. Nor is this out of any contempt for semantic inquiries in general, but because the New Testament usage provides no more than the very beginnings of an answer to the problems raised by the concept of the kerygma today, and does not in any sense give a thought-out account of the kerygma. For the rest, the hermeneutic problems raised in attempting to form historiographical and systematic theological concepts are so complex that it is hardly wise to content oneself with adopting New Testament usage.[25] The extraordinary importance of Bultmann's conception of the kerygma seems to me to be seen most clearly at this point: it is that he has thought out the internal relationship of that which one might more superficially distinguish as the formal and material sense of the concept. He poses the question: How far are the main issues concerning Christian faith inseparably tied to a particular understanding of the word-event?

According to Bultmann we are concerned in the kerygma, not in the first place with the imparting of information, but with a challenge which demands from us obedience and decision,[26] and which is addressed to the will[27] or, to be more precise, to the conscience.[28] The kerygma, thus seen as a challenge, qualifies anew the situation of the man to whom it is addressed.[29] That is to say, that the kerygma considered as Word is an event which overtakes the man who hears it and forces him to a decision between faith and unfaith, and consequently to a decision about his own understanding of himself.[30] The kerygma which presents man with a choice between faith and unfaith is the kerygma which tells of the particular eschatological act of God in Jesus Christ,[31] i.e. of the paradox of the eschaton appearing in time.[32] For as eschatological address the kerygma as challenge is identical with the content of the kerygma: the eschatological event which takes place within the relationship of Word and faith. In this way the unity of the two sides of the problem which we have sketched out can be preserved in the concept of the kerygma.

Jesus' proclamation, as to a lesser degree prophetic speech,[33] has characteristics which correspond to this concept of the kerygma. This is true of its 'challenge and response' character, but also of its eschatological qualification. Only here the difference becomes clear between the proclamation of Jesus and that of primitive Christianity, which latter only is properly to be called kerygma, because its reference is to the eschatological act of God which has already taken place.[34] Hence kerygma in the strict sense of the word, is christological kerygma, which the proclamation of Jesus[35] was of course not. Moreover, as the christological kerygma it is the Word of God itself, although of course it is possible for other words which are not in the first place kerygma to be, in an indirect sense, God's Word.[36] Only even here we must still consider their relation to the kerygma.

We must postpone answering many of the questions raised by such a brief account of Bultmann's position, in order to concentrate on the question: how do we come to understand the kerygma as kerygma? In this we must take for granted Bultmann's assumption that it will not do to try and avoid the question by invoking the aid of the Holy Spirit too early in the discussion. It soon becomes clear that the question of understanding the kerygma as kerygma is closely intertwined with the complex hermeneutic problems raised by the relation of historical and dogmatic speech. It might be said that Bultmann's great contribution to this history of theology lies in the fact that he has concentrated so much attention on this relationship. It is therefore not surprising that it is at precisely this key-point that further questions will be raised for those who seek to advance the cause of theology by the study of hermeneutics.

Although Bultmann in his use of the word kerygma is concerned primarily with the formation of concepts for systematic theology, his work as an exegete never allows him to lose sight of the fact that the kerygma is an historical entity. After what we have said above, it may seem strange that we should express this in a concessive clause. The very nature of the subject demands that the proclamation here and now should be orientated on what was kerygma then. How then can we properly understand the connection between the two? In his use of the term 'kerygma', Bultmann is in the first place concerned to stress the character of the proclamation as address, that is, as event. That speech about the 'fact' of Jesus Christ is constitutive for the kerygma should not be seen as being in opposition to this, but rather as being constitutive of the character of the kerygma as 'word-event'. The That of the saving fact corresponds to the 'that' of its proclamation. To put it more precisely: together they form a single fact.[37] Yet even if we accept this, there still remains the question of the relationship between the kerygma which has been handed down and the kerygma which we must now proclaim, and we should be careful to distinguish this relationship from the one we have just sketched between the proclaimed fact (Jesus Christ) and the fact of the proclamation (kerygma). It is the nature of the kerygma that it is an address made here and now, that is, that the event-character is of the 'essence' of the address; and so it follows that kerygma which is handed down cannot, in so far as it is handed down, be kerygma. It has been kerygma. For just that reason it is not actual kerygma.

It does not follow that we should therefore attach less value to past kerygma. On the contrary, it is its task to ratify and to purify actual kerygma. One can only understand the import of the kerygma which is handed down to us if we bear in mind the distinction between kerygma in an historical sense, and kerygma in an actual sense; for only this distinction reveals the full force of the tension within the concept of kerygma. One can attribute all the above-mentioned 'structural moments' to the kerygma—its character as address, its relation to a fact which is not merely the subject of an historical report, but is also witnessed to here and now—and still represent it as the historical interpretation of kerygma which has been handed down, which has already taken place. It is not merely because he happens to be a New Testament scholar that Bultmann reaches his concept of the kerygma by an analysis of the kerygmatic tradition contained in the New Testament; it is because this orientation of the kerygma on the New Testament tradition is theologically the only legitimate method of procedure. It is by this method that the structure of present, actual kerygma can be worked out, and this is something which obviously has more than a merely historical relevance. Yet, while linguistically its function is limited to repeating or alternatively to summarising the kerygmatic christological formulations of primitive Christianity,[38] one must always bear in mind that just because these formulations have been kerygma and because they are undoubtedly indispensable for pointing the way to new kerygma, this does not mean that they are necessarily themselves kerygma. Rather, we should beware of the danger of allowing theological discussion of the kerygma to content itself simply with summarising the kerygma in terms of traditional kerygmatic formulations. This may well lead us to neglect the nature of the kerygma as 'word-event'. It may mean that the (historical!) summary undoes the work of the historical analysis of the kerygma, which was to show it as an address which is actually being made. It may be tempting in New Testament studies to concentrate on the relationship between the proclaimed fact (Jesus Christ) to the fact of the proclamation (the kerygma): but for dogmatics this is to oversimplify very dangerously. Any discussion of the concept of kerygma must take into account not only the above-mentioned relationship, but the relationship which is decisive for the progress of the kerygma, namely the relationship between the inherited kerygma of the past and kerygma which is actually taking place.[39]

Now it may indeed seem out of place in a discussion of Bultmann to insist on the necessity of interpreting traditional formulae. It is by no means my intention to accuse him of neglecting the very thing he has so often reminded us of. If one takes his work as a whole, then the details which we have just brought out will be seen as unmistakably a part of that work. Yet perhaps it is not superfluous to emphasise potential sources of danger which may arise if one fails to pay attention to the distinction between kerygma in its historical sense and its actual sense.

The distinction which Bultmann draws between theology and kerygma allows criticism of theology while insuring the kerygma against it.[40] Yet it would be to misunderstand Bultmann's position if one were to take 'kerygma' here as referring to particular traditional formulations which, in contra-distinction to theological elaboration, are immune from criticism; this, even if the way in which he usually characterises the kerygma, might easily lead us into such a misconception. For of course kerygmatic formulae always contain certain elements of theological interpretation.[41] Not that these are as such necessarily false. 'Criticism' in this case is seen as an interpretation which brings out clearly the sense of the theologoumena. This of course means refusing to by-pass the differences in language which make their understanding so difficult. In other words it means taking the historical character of the traditional text seriously.

For this reason the principle that one may not inquire back behind the kerygma[42] is in no way intended to apply to traditional kerygmatic formulations seen simply as historical texts. For this would be to close the door on the interpretation of kerygmatic tradition and to turn the authority of the Word of God into a *sacrificium intellectus* to a *fides historica* (which may of course also have dogmatic content).

Thus even if we characterise faith as the acceptance of the Christian kerygma, as faith in the kerygma and as faith directed towards the kerygma,[43] we must in the last resort go on to make this more explicit. We must show that the Word on which faith fastens is not merely a particular christological formula which has become the object of historical knowledge, but is an address which arouses faith and which is made to men with a particular outlook and understanding. This is in no way to say that traditional formulae may not assume kerygmatic character in an actual sense, only that we must not neglect the hermeneutic distinction which this implies, however small it may seem to be. This is fundamentally the same point, here made with regard to the relation of the kerygma to the Word of God, which we have made elsewhere in discussing the orthodox doctrine of the relation of Scripture to the Word of God.[44]

However, this distinction has consequences which reach far beyond these basically very minor points. Now, to be sure, it is true that the kerygma is handed down and preserved in certain fixed forms of words;[45] and this fact is of great importance when we reflect on the nature of the kerygma. But this tendency towards certain fixed formulae must in no way be equated with either the proclamatory character of the kerygma or the process of proclaiming it again, although it is related to both of them. Of course the proclamation of Christ, true to its nature as an eschatological message—in contra-distinction e.g. to the instruction of mystical or moralistic world-views—tends most naturally to find expression in the briefest confessional formulations, e.g. the acclamations 'Jesus Christ' or *kyrios Iēsous*. The peculiarity of this linguistic event is related to the particular understanding of time which the kerygma implies. We are only justified in calling such formulations kerygmatic[46] because in them we are directed to the ground of the kerygma. This always, however, with the reservation that these formulations, in so far as they merely preserve the kerygma, are not kerygma in the proper sense of an address made here and now.

There has been a tendency, with regard to this aspect of the concrete event of proclamation, to link the word kerygma with mission, and to distinguish mission from the different situation within the congregation by drawing the distinction between missionary preaching and congregational preaching or between kērygma and didachē.[47] We do not wish here to go into the historical question of how these terms were used in primitive Christianity, or even to pass judgment on the correctness of such a distinction. Yet one can still say of the kerygma in missionary preaching that, no matter how much its full import was brought out in those kerygmatic formulae (whose *paradosis* played an important part in the missionary activity of the church), it can hardly be said itself to have consisted merely in the direct retailing of such formulae without further explanation. The same is true of the situation in the congregation, where of course, in so far as proclamation in some way continued to play a part, people were not prepared to rest content with the mere repetition of kerygmatic formulae.

It has been said that *pisteuein* in the New Testament often has the sense of coming to faith, meaning by this the 'acceptance of the Christian kerygma', and that it belongs in the first place to 'missionary terminology'.[48] Yet even though this is accurate as an analysis of the use of the term, it may give a distorted picture of its actual content, suggesting that the kerygmatic formula as such awoke faith,[49] whereas on the contrary the faith which had been awoken made the kerygmatic formulae its own. If we persist in identifying the kerygma with a particular formula, then the phrase 'faith in the kerygma' is inaccurate. Even if we see the kerygma as something actual, the formulation 'faith in the kerygma' is still improper, however much faith draws its life from the Word of proclamation. The preposition *eis* when used in the New Testament with *pisteuein* and *pistis*, as near as makes no difference, always qualifies Jesus Christ and not *kērygma, euaggelion* etc.[50] This should show the impossibility of maintaining that the tradition of kerygmatic formulae is to be equated with proclamation itself, however much these formulae, properly used, may be valuable as aids in ensuring that the kerygma remains kerygma.

We must take this a step further. Even if the kerygma is not normally and in principle achieved merely by presenting a traditional kerygmatic formula, we must still hold fast to the basic definition of the kerygma as christological kerygma. The kerygma does indeed allow, as the diversity of the New Testament well shows, a great variety in the different christological forms in which it is presented. It not only allows this, but it is necessary that, since it is to be proclaimed throughout history, it should be expressed with the help of differing Christologies. H. Braun attempts to solve the problem which this presents for the unity of the New Testament when he says that the self-understanding of faith is the constant and the Christology the variable.[51] But rather than asking the further question about the possible limits of the unity of the self-understanding of faith in the New Testament witnesses, and also about the actual limits of the legitimate variations in Christology, it is more important to make the following observation. Even if one can speak of Christology as being variable in its form, it still seems to be a mark of the constant of the self-understanding of faith, that the faith is faith in Jesus Christ, that is, faith which is directed to the christological kerygma, and which accepts this kerygma in its own confession. Using Braun's terminology we could say: Because and in so far as the self-understanding of faith is the constant, Christology is indeed variable in the way it is expressed (in its How) but not in the fact that it is expressed (in its That). There is no choice—and this is for the sake of the self-understanding of faith—between, for example, christological and non-christological kerygma.

This brings us nearer to the heart of the question about the understanding of the kerygma as kerygma. If we have to deal with the kerygma only as christological kerygma, then the fact of its variability may in some way make it easier for us to understand it. But the christological structure of the kerygma as such is so much a genuine product of primitive Christianity, that in proclaiming the christological kerygma one clearly can not avoid using traditional kerygmatic formulae, either in the form of christological titles or of christological event-statements. This again raises great problems of interpretation. The situation in the earliest days of Christianity or in the following centuries may well have been more favourable to the understanding of the basic christological statements of the kerygma; but today we cannot avoid the difficulties to which they give rise. One cannot avoid the overwhelming impression that today at any rate the christological titles and the kerygmatic event-statements are very foreign indeed to those who are not used to them and to those who, in spite of their long acquaintance with them, are called on to give a responsible account of them.

So it seems that precisely those formulae which ought to give most cogent expression to the faith, do, in fact, make it more difficult to understand. The content of the faith presented in the kerygmatic formulae does not provide us, at least in this form, with a basis of faith. It is no mere chance that the question of the basis of faith so easily turns into a question about proofs. If the kerygma is not in itself intelligible, then either it must presuppose and demand a faith which already has its basis in something other than the kerygma; or else we must examine the basis of the kerygma in an attempt to show that it is the same as the basis of faith. We may not at this point appeal to the scandal of the kerygma as an excuse for our inability to render it intelligible. Kerygma which is unintelligible conceals the true scandal and causes offence in the wrong way. As such it fails to call men to decision.[52] When we seek to understand the kerygma as kerygma, we are concerned simply with this one question: how it is to be proclaimed as the scandal of truth, which passes judgment on reality and becomes intelligible, not because its kerygmatic character is resolved, but rather because this has been given full emphasis.

Now of course everyone is agreed that the traditional kerygmatic formulae need to be interpreted for those to whom we preach today. But what does this mean? It means that we have to give some account of the various linguistic elements, e.g. the christological titles, which traditional kerygma has employed and which come from a world which is no longer our own. A thorough-going interpretation will have to examine the historical origins of these titles, *christos, kyrios, uios tou theou*, etc., not indeed with the intention of presenting them as strange historical curiosities, but in order to show the self-understanding which is expressed in them (by which is meant the comprehensive understanding of reality which they embody). Every christological title represents a particular interpretation of reality, and this means in concrete terms a particular understanding of the way in which man is claimed, questioned, threatened and given hope.

This task of interpreting traditional kerygmatic formulations brings with it its own set of difficulties. Even if we could bring such an interpretation to a successful conclusion, it would not dispel the great difference which exists between an age in which these christological titles together with the understanding of reality which they express were to be found in non-christian use, and an age in which they are to be found only as titles which have survived from former times and this only in their christian use. Whereas once they had the task of bringing out the importance of Jesus' appearance, today they must themselves first be interpreted, before they can fulfil their task of interpreting Jesus. In so far as we have to deal here with mythological concepts—and these are to be found to a greater or lesser extent in all christological language—there has again been a significant change in emphasis. Whereas before, certain of the existing mythological concepts were claimed by the kerygma, we now have to make mythological concepts our own for the sake of the kerygma. Whereas once the impact of the kerygma on mythological language served in some sense to demythologise it, what strikes us today about the kerygma is that it seems to demand that we mythologise our language.

We must then attempt an interpretation of christological titles by bringing out the understanding of reality which we find expressed in them. Such an attempt may in part uncover the true situation of men today, and thus help to bring home to men the claims on them which are expressed in the titles. But it will also make demands on us which we will not be able to meet. This the more so, since the role which the christological titles have to play in interpreting the kerygma is clearly limited. Of course they are intended to say who Jesus is, with regard to the reality which we experience; but then every interpretation of reality claims to explain reality which has been experienced, although it seems obliged to do this by means of statements which perhaps necessarily refuse to be reduced to the level of experience! But if these titles do claim to say who Jesus is, then they must be submitted to a radical reinterpretation. For the meaning of *christos*, *kyrios*, *uios tou theou*, etc., when applied to Jesus, is not immediately obvious from the then existing use of these terms—which is by no means to suggest that the existing use is of no consequence for the interpretation. Rather, they only receive a definite meaning when they are applied to Jesus. By comparison with their original sense they are all to some extent transformed through their being applied to Jesus. It is just this process of reinterpretation which represents the decisive kerygmatic event in such statements about Jesus. What is the point then of creating a situation where we have to reinterpret titles which we have contrived to make our own? Doesn't the situation lack the urgency which we need to convince us of its importance?

Now we may be able to overcome the objections which are raised partly with regard to the historicity of the kerygma—which seems to make it incumbent on us to remain constant to the memory of certain linguistic forms—and partly with regard to the programme of existential interpretation of these christological titles, which can in fact give great assistance to present proclamation. But even then the question remains: how can we come to a right understanding of the kerygma expressed in the traditional christological language *as kerygma*? The question here seems to me two-fold. Firstly with regard to particular kerygmatic statements which need to be interpreted in the way we have suggested, before they become clear. This can in no way be achieved by means of the christological titles or other expressions alone. Statements such as 'Jesus is Christ' or 'Jesus is risen' cannot be fully interpreted merely by examining their predicates. Even if one interprets all that is predicated of Jesus with reference to the eschatological event as the lowest common denominator[53] it still remains unclear what this means, if we leave out of account the fact that they are intended as statements about *Jesus.* Only by reference to him can the meaning of the predicates themselves become clear.

But this leads one on to a further consideration. How does it ever happen that kerygma, with whatever titles and expressions, comes into existence at all? There were eschatological ideas independent of Jesus, before he even lived. But in themselves they do not produce kerygma. If the use of the name of Jesus is not to be arbitrary and meaningless, then we must clearly find in it an indication of what it is that compels men and gives them the right to use existing eschatological language for the kerygma, and in so doing to define eschatology with reference to the kerygma. The decisive thing about the kerygma is not that there were certain views of reality to hand with whose help men could attempt to express what had happened in Jesus. The decisive thing is the appearance of a challenge qualifying the situation of men and authorising them to deliver the kerygma; which not only makes kerygmatic statements intelligible in their particular concrete form, but also explains the necessity of kerygma at all, and so enables us to understand kerygma as kerygma.

In this way the problem of the intelligibility of the kerygma is viewed in a new light and can be seen to require a discussion in terms of more than just that of interpretation—at any rate in the usual sense of the word. The interpretation of particular kerygmatic formulations is not enough. Until we have become clear about the necessity of kerygmatic statements in themselves, we will achieve nothing more than an historical (*historisch*) understanding. The decisive problem of proclamation is no longer the unintelligibility of particular kerygmatic utterances, which can in the end be interpreted, however difficult such a task may prove to be. It is rather the lack of understanding with regard to the christological kerygma as such; it is that men no longer feel that it has any claim on them, that they no longer understand what it is to be gripped by the eschaton, and that for this reason christological kerygma has become meaningless. But can the traditional christological kerygma meet this situation in such a way that it can be recognised as an essential ingredient of it and be capable of restating the situation itself?

Now doubtless the interpretation of traditional kerygmatic statements is not in itself kerygma.[54] It would be quite wrong to think that the task of proclamation today consists simply in interpreting traditional kerygma. Even the theological business of Christology is not exhausted by the mere interpretation of traditional Christology. It is two-fold: to interpret the traditional kerygma and then, guided by this interpretation, to carry out the *kērussein* itself. This task assumes that the preacher has himself felt the claims of the 'event' from which the christological kerygma derives its necessity. It consists in addressing one's listeners in such a way that they begin to see their situation is determined by the ground of the christological kerygma and to see in what way it is determined. It consists in showing them that in this sense, i.e. not on the strength of a postulate but of a direct confrontation, the christological kerygma is necessary for them.

If kerygma is to be understood as kerygma then it is of urgent concern to inquire in what situation kerygma can be understood as kerygma. The question sounds dangerous. For on the one hand the kerygma seems valid for every man in every situation. On the other hand the kerygma seems to qualify every situation in such a way that it becomes kerygmatic, i.e. that it becomes a situation in which kerygma is necessary, in which therefore it can be understood as kerygma. But against this it should be pointed out that the traditional christological kerygma seems to assume a situation which is already qualified as a kerygmatic situation. It presupposes faith. It does indeed point to the place where faith has its ground, but as christological kerygma is not itself the ground of faith.

Now if we carry this line of thought a stage further, we see that we must introduce a further distinction with regard to the kerygma. It becomes clear that traditional christological kerygma possesses something which is in a specific sense kerygma, but is not in the traditional sense christological kerygma. Moreover, it should help to get the matter straight if we keep in mind the question about the kerygmatic situation. By this I do not simply mean any situation which exists when christological kerygma happens to be made. Rather I mean the specific situation which must be discovered and brought to life in the actual situation of the hearer and must thus be shown as the true situation. It is this which makes christological kerygma meaningful and in this sense one could speak of proclamation producing the kerygmatic situation.

If we are to be able to answer for christological kerygma, then we should not attempt to induce christological ideas and concepts in ourselves and others by means of suggestion. The decisive thing is that we should be able to use Christology as a manner of speech which is relevant to our situation. There can be no question here of retreating from our actual situation into a religious corner where the kerygmatic situation can still be preserved or restored. The truth of the christological kerygma depends on the truth of the proposition that the situation in which we actually find ourselves at any given moment is at bottom, though perhaps in a very hidden way, a kerygmatic situation. It is this which verifies christological kerygma. For we cannot be content with a positivism based on traditional christological kerygma, but must persevere with the question of the basis of faith as the question: What is it that constitutes the situation in which the kerygma is understood as kerygma, i.e. in which the necessity of the kerygma is understood?

3. The historical Jesus

At this point, it becomes necessary to speak of Jesus. Our reflections on the kerygma have led to this in two ways. Firstly we saw that the clarity (*Eindeutigkeit*) of christological statements depends on their being understood as statements about Jesus. And further we noticed that the intelligibility of christological statements depends on the situation being qualified as kerygmatic, i.e. depends on that which constitutes the basis and the necessity of the christological kerygma. Now the christological kerygma itself points us most clearly to this basis. One cannot escape the persistence with which it uses the name of Jesus. Nor is this only because the kerygma happens to make christological statements about Jesus, it is also—and this is really one and the same thing—because it constantly claims Jesus as its authority. (We shall of course still have to see how it does this.) Prepositional phrases such as *eis Iēsoun Christon, dia Iēsou Christou, dia Iēsoun Christon, en Iēsou Christōi,* and corresponding constructions with *onoma Iēsou Christou* give ample evidence of this.

The fact that it has now become necessary to speak about Jesus in order to uphold the kerygma has been in great measure responsible for theology's return to the new[1] quest for the historical Jesus. This has in fact taken place on a very large scale[2] even though no adequate account has been given of the reasons which make it necessary and justifiable to turn away from Bultmann's own position. One can scarcely maintain that the discovery of new sources or the development of new methods of study give adequate historical grounds for this change in the course of theology. I think that it is much rather the necessity of such a search from the point of view of hermeneutics which has proved decisive. The search for the historical Jesus is a search for the hermeneutic key to Christology.[3]

I shall therefore be concerned expressly with the relation of the quest for the historical Jesus to systematic theology. For it seems to me that it is not only the present renewed discussion of the historical Jesus, which has its roots in systematic theology (even if this is not always recognised), but that it was and always will be the case that men's search for Jesus, consciously or unconsciously, directly or indirectly, has a bearing on dogmatics, and produces decisive results for its study.[4] It is simply the case that whenever Jesus becomes the subject of study, it is at the same time theology which is being studied. It was simply in accordance with the state of the discussion that the new departure in the quest for the historical Jesus should spring from dogmatic interests[5] and that interpretation should be guided by knowledge of the primitive christian kerygma,[6] and as such this can scarcely give grounds for criticism. Yet this gives one no grounds for supposing that one is absolved by one's dogmatic programme from the task of dealing carefully with historical questions, i.e. from historical and critical reflection on the contribution of historical study to theology. Bultmann, as perhaps no other theologian, combines a masterly skill in the use of the historical critical methods with revolutionary thought in systematic theology; yet one can still find remarks where the two stand together quite unrelated to each other, where the only possible justification for such remarks can be that they do at least attack a false relationship between history and dogmatics.[7]

Now of course as far as the historical quest for Jesus is concerned there are obviously certain things which it would be quite pointless to try to prove. We shall hardly prove Jesus' messiahship by demonstrating his messianic consciousness; we shall not be able to get back behind the message of his resurrection to prove the historical fact on which it rests; nor will we be able to show by means of any other 'objectively demonstrable' facts in Jesus' ministry, that he was the Son of God or that he died for us. Quite apart from the questions of historical detail which this raises, such a procedure would run counter to the logic of historical judgments. Messianic consciousness says nothing about actual messiahship. The resurrection of which the kerygma speaks, that is an eschatological resurrection and not merely a temporary reanimation, is by definition not an historical fact.[8] An historical proof of the fact of Jesus' Sonship would obliterate the distinction between Sonship of God as a phenomenon in the history of religions and the kerygmatic sense which it has when predicated of Jesus. And apart from the impossibility of making historically valid judgments about Jesus' own attitude to his death,[9] knowing *his* attitude to it would still not relieve *me* of the responsibility of deciding how I myself stand in relation to it.

Bultmann has declared that any attempt to get back behind the kerygma[10] is illegitimate. Now it is true that such an enquiry may be conducted either for the purposes of giving a dogmatic account of the nature of the kerygma or as a means of interpreting traditional kerygma; nor is it easy to draw a line[11] between these two alternatives. Yet as soon as we examine the kerygma as an historical phenomenon,[12] that is in the form of particular texts which have been handed down, it becomes pointless to forbid the attempt to get back behind the texts, whether it be to try to get back behind the Pauline kerygma to the kerygma of the primitive community, or to get back behind this to the kerygma of Jesus himself. It is of course quite right to be concerned to see that the manner in which we attempt to get back behind the text is appropriate to the subject matter. We may even perhaps see Bultmann's ban on such attempts as a warning against the wish to be able to prove the kerygma, the impropriety of which we have just discussed. But it is one thing to give a warning against improper attempts to get back behind the kerygma in order to provide a *'legitimation'* for it; it is quite another to stress the necessity of such attempts for the purpose of *interpretation*. Here we must leave on one side the question whether or not it is possible to see the attempt to legitimate the kerygma in a different way which might be appropriate to the matter in hand[13] and which would then be identical with the question of its interpretation.

It depends of course on the way in which such an interpretation is undertaken. Bultmann has always attacked the positivist idea of history as well as the attempt to by-pass it with a dualism of method. But even so one has the impression that he has not reflected deeply enough on the problem. The way in which the historical critical method has been pursued in the past may indeed give grounds for supposing that it is tied to the ascertainment of objectively demonstrable facts.[14] Such a narrow understanding of the method seems to me dangerous, for it sets a gulf between it and existential interpretation;[15] I would rather suggest that where such interpretation is properly applied, it must be given its due place within the historical critical method. This would mean that the attempt to get back behind the kerygma is by no means necessarily an attempt only to get back to objective facts, but also, in so far as the subject allows and demands, to get back to that which has 'come to expression' in the kerygma.[16] In this way the observation of linguistic events[17] may also be undertaken from the point of view of historical fact, but in such a way that what is perceived may not simply be dealt with as a speechless fact, but compels one to seek the 'word-event' which springs from it. If one only has objective facts in mind when one talks about getting back behind the kerygma, then one will hardly do justice to the questions we are dealing with here. For if one has to do with Jesus, one has to do not with mere facts but with pure Word.[18] If we carry out our attempts to get back behind the primitive christian kerygma in a proper manner, then we shall not be looking for facts which confirm the Word, but we shall be looking beyond a word which needs interpretation for the word-event which is presupposed within it.

Bultmann divides the question of the 'Relation of the Primitive Christian message of Christ to the Historical Jesus' under two heads: 'the question of the *historical continuity* of the work of the historical Jesus (and here particular emphasis is laid on his preaching) with the early christian kerygma of Christ', and the question of the *material relation* of Jesus and the kerygma.[19] He considers one of the chief faults of present discussion to be that these two questions are not clearly distinguished, with the result that it seems that the second question has been answered when we have in fact only answered the first.[20] Now of course the two questions are closely related. Before we can approach the problem of the *historical continuity*, we need to give some preliminary definition of the 'difference between the historical Jesus and the kerygma of Christ,'[21] and that means an equally provisional definition of the material relation between the two. The problem of the continuity cannot be discussed at all without mention of the material relationship.[22]

This entanglement of the two questions is of course just what we should expect. For if in its historical application we are to avoid formalising the category of continuity[23] into the old scientific concept of a space-time continuum, then we must have in mind some material relationship which embraces both identity and difference. Unless one prefers simply to abandon the terminology of 'discontinuity' and 'continuity',[24] one must at least be clear in one's mind that historical continuity always includes identity and difference, whereas discontinuity in the absolute sense of complete disparity simply puts an end to historical enquiry. Normally what one means by discontinuity is: that of two events, where one follows on the other the difference between the two is not deducible from the first, in spite of the connection which obtains between them. In other words it is a 'discontinuity' only observed within a certain continuity, and which modifies this continuity. This terminology is unsatisfactory because in it either continuity or discontinuity are not seen as real alternatives but stand in a dialectical relationship to one another, in such a way that they can be predicated of every sequence of events, and as such already give expression to a material relationship; or else they are conceived so formally that continuity as the mere fact of sequence in time and space says nothing about the nature of the relationship of the events. In this case continuity remains historically unimportant until the actual nature of the relationship is considered, and until one has also reflected on the character of such a 'sequence', when it is predicated of historical (*geschichtlich*) and not merely physical relationships.[25]

It is therefore significant that Bultmann both affirms the historical continuity between Jesus and the kerygma, and at the same time passes it over as of little importance.[26] But the way in which he expresses the obvious fact of this continuity, which he would see simply as the contingency between the kerygma and the mere That of the historicity of Jesus, cries out for an explanation in terms of a material relationship. It may be 'obvious' that 'the kerygma presupposes the historical Jesus'. It is by no means obvious, however, what is meant by this. What is the meaning and content of 'presupposition' here? Clearly the sentence, 'Without Jesus there would be no kerygma', is unexceptionable, as long as one is only concerned with the mere fact that the name of Jesus is constitutive for the primitive christian kerygma. But as soon as one inquires into the meaning of the sentence, 'Without him there would have been no kerygma', one is faced *in nuce* with the *whole* problem of the relation between Jesus and the primitive christian kerygma.[27] The idea that one can deal with the problem of the historical continuity apart from the problem of the material relationship is based on the reduction of the relation between Jesus and the primitive christian kerygma to the simple relevance of the mere 'That' of Jesus' person—and this we shall question later. Yet even though Bultmann accepts a 'continuity' only in this sense, the question of the material relationship is still not without substance for him. It is not clear, however, how, if one disregards the historical (*geschichtlich*) nature of this material relationship, it can properly be discussed in terms of a comparison of the purely ideal structures of two different types of self-understanding. What emerges from this is that Bultmann himself has more to say about the relation of Jesus to the primitive christian kerygma than one would expect from one occupying his own fundamental position with regard to the question.

First, we should notice that Bultmann tells us very little about the theological significance of the quest for the historical Jesus in relation to the two questions which he poses. On principle he is quite right to regard 'the question as a purely historical one'.[28] But this emphasis seems to indicate that the historical question has no theological relevance and that any theological interest in it is to be regarded with suspicion. Bultmann himself has only a polemical interest in the question and is only concerned to repudiate its theological relevance. There is a similarity between Bultmann's polemical position with regard to the quest for the historical Jesus, and that of the liberal search for the historical Jesus which was interested in 'demonstrating the difference between Jesus and the kerygma.'[29] Yet, unlike the liberals, Bultmann sees this not as a criticism of the kerygma, but as a means of bringing out its particular character. His polemic is directed against all attempts (liberal or positivist) to permit any question concerning the historical Jesus to be considered as theologically relevant to the kerygma.

In Bultmann's view the new state of the discussion has been brought about by men's interest in 'elaborating the unity of the historical Jesus and the Christ of the kerygma,'[30] and this—*cum grano salis*—is true enough. Yet the concept of unity is highly complex and in this case in no way seems to stand in contradiction to the difference between the historical Jesus and the kerygma of Christ. Rather it means that we cannot simply rest content with recording the difference, but must tackle the further task of interpreting this difference with regard to the fact that the kerygma at least claims the name of Jesus for itself. Yet Bultmann impugns the value of this point of view by the suggestion that there is an illegitimate apologetic interest at work here.[31]

On the other hand, since one cannot deny the possibility of the historical quest for Jesus, one can indeed 'come some way towards meeting such attempts.'[32] But in Bultmann's view the most that will come out of it, i.e. if one attempts an existential interpretation of the proclamation and ministry of Jesus, is a dilemma, and so in effect Bultmann merely draws more capital from the quest for the historical Jesus for his own theological polemic. For the success of such an interpretation would seem to enter into competition with the kerygma and in the end to make it superfluous.[33] Admittedly, such a view is mere illusion according to Bultmann. For it is only in the kerygma that Jesus is present as the eschatological event.[34] Thus Bultmann has no theological reason with regard to the kerygma for embarking on the new quest. Bultmann is prepared to give a critical discussion of the quest, but only—and this is yet another remarkable exchange of roles[35]—as an apologetic for the kerygma against those who maintain that the kerygma stands in need of an apologetic which can be furnished by a positive assessment of the quest for the historical Jesus.

Now there are in fact two very closely connected theological reasons (which Bultmann seems to overlook), which do indeed provide strong arguments for the theological necessity of the quest for the historical Jesus. In the first place the mere fact that the kerygma speaks of Jesus, imposes a strong obligation on the theologian to take this speech about a historical person seriously by making an enquiry into his personal history. Now one may say that this is in no way a specifically theological reason but merely corresponds to an historical tendency of thought which insists that we examine historically everything which is patient of such an examination. Indeed, this is not a specifically theological attitude but is rather the expression of an interest which may have nothing to do with theology. Yet it is specifically theological to think conscientiously, even as a theologian. This means that whoever feels inescapably bound to an historical way of thought—and this is true of all modern men, no matter how much they may try to avoid it—must, even if he is a theologian, meet such an obligation by taking historical phenomena seriously as *historical*. This obligation is *theological*, regardless of the particular results it may yield for theology. For whatever happens it will be seen as a weakness on the part of a theologian if he fails to meet such an obligation. Nor is it legitimate to raise the objection that primitive Christianity and countless generations thereafter did not raise the question of the historical Jesus, at least not in the critical manner of modern historians. Nor is it any excuse to point out that the kerygma itself does not even speak of Jesus as an historical phenomenon, at least, that is, that in speaking of him it betrays no specific historical interest. Yet it does speak of God with relation to Jesus, and Jesus was an historical person. This point is of such decisive importance for the kerygma that we shall have to put particular emphasis on it despite the fact that our manner of doing so may seem far removed from the primitive christian kerygma.[36]

The other consideration which shows the theological necessity of the quest for the historical Jesus follows on from the first. It concerns the interpretation of the primitive christian kerygma. Now one should not allow oneself to be misled by the category of continuity into attempting to give a causal explanation of the relation of Jesus and the primitive christian kerygma, thinking thereby that one can give a proof of the latter.[37] To be sure one must ask how Jesus' life and preaching lead to the development of the primitive christian kerygma. But unless one attempts a careful interpretation of such phenomena, with regard to their historical relationships, there will always be the danger of short-circuiting the real historical problems, with possibly disastrous consequences for theology; this, whether one seeks to prove that Jesus already taught the basic outlines of the kerygma,[38] or whether one tries to show the difference between the kerygma and Jesus' proclamation by pointing to the new facts on which the former depended, i.e. the resurrection of Jesus,[39] understood as a fact additional to the ministry of Jesus, or alternatively to any other creative religious processes within the primitive community.

In the first place it is the primitive christian kerygma which we have to interpret, for this is in an historical sense primary. Yet the way in which the kerygma concentrates attention on the name of Jesus, that is to say on his person, poses the question to what extent the kerygmatic statements about Jesus, or rather the faith in him which they express, are grounded in him. Even if the kerygma does not make this clear by giving historical details, it nevertheless insists on the indispensable importance of his person. This leaves us with the following tasks in the interpretation of the kerygma. If we could ascertain nothing historically authentic concerning the person to whom the kerygma refers, then the relation of Jesus to the kerygma would consist in nothing more than in a series of assertions for the understanding of which Jesus himself would have no more importance than that of a random and meaningless cipher. In this sense the kerygma, if such it could be called, would be no more than a mere myth. Nor would the matter be basically any different if all we could discover about Jesus—in so far as an abstraction of this sort is at all conceivable with historical events—was the mere fact of the existence at a certain time and place of an otherwise completely unknown person by the name of Jesus.[40]

This is in fact far from being the case. By contrast with the possibilities which we have outlined above, which allow no concrete distinction between Jesus himself and the statements of the kerygma about him, we can at least be sure of one thing: it is that we can discover a concrete difference between them, i.e. that the historical Jesus not only can be, but must be distinguished from the kerygma. The assessment of this difference will therefore be a necessary part of the interpretation of the kerygma. In the first place we shall have to see whether this difference is in the nature of a contradiction or even one of complete disparity. Nor should one object that such a question is improper with regard to the kerygma. For seeing that the name of Jesus is a component of the kerygma, the kerygma must be open to everything which Jesus represents and which his name makes explicit. Any attempt to lay down prohibitions at this point, or to insist that the kerygma cannot be affected by such questions, would be to insinuate that the kerygma does not take the name of Jesus seriously and that it flees the light of intelligible speech by taking refuge in the obscurity of his name. Now if the difference between Jesus and the kerygma should turn out to be in the nature of an absolute contradiction, and, as such, to be a startling misinterpretation of Jesus, or if it turned out that although the kerygma uses the name of Jesus it completely misses the point, then the kerygma would have cancelled itself out as a self-contradiction.[41] For it is not intended to contradict Jesus but to correspond to him. It is not meant to pass him over, but to let him alone count. That is in fact its real concern.

If we discount these extreme and theoretical limiting cases, i.e. that it could be shown that the kerygma either contradicts or completely by-passes the historical Jesus, then we see how the quest for Jesus is of central importance for the interpretation of the kerygma. The two main points have already emerged in our discussion of the nature of the kerygma. Firstly: the linguistic elements in the kerygmatic statements are not in themselves unambiguous, but only become so when they are predicated of Jesus. Even though, for example, the christological titles should interpret Jesus, they must at the same time be interpreted in the light of Jesus.[42] Secondly: the fact of the kerygma must be understood in the light of him through whom it became an event, through whom it gained its charter, its legitimation. The mention of Jesus' name in the kerygma serves not only to indicate the content of the kerygma, but also to indicate its basis.[43] Now this point is of importance for the understanding of the kerygma as kerygma. It is also important because of the variability of the kerygmatic formulations. However simple it may sound, we must stress in the first place—while still holding fast to the description of the self-understanding of faith as the constant[44]—that the proclamation of the name of Jesus is the common element in all the variability of the kerygma. The kerygma itself names Jesus as its criterion.

Now at this point there are two reservations which we should make about the theological necessity of the quest for the historical Jesus. We have been concerned with the theoretical development of the problem, and of course it remains to be seen what light the question of the historical Jesus actually sheds on theology. Again, so far we have only been considering the historical quest from the point of view of the necessity of such a quest for the interpretation of the *primitive christian* kerygma. No one will wish to deny that we can speak of the necessity of this quest as a theological necessity. Yet we shall only discover its full significance if we are not prepared to rest content with determining the importance of this quest for the interpretation of the primitive christian kerygma. For we must go on to put the further question which belongs to the sphere of systematic theology, about the necessity of speaking of the historical Jesus for our proclamation of Christ *today*.

First, however, we must ask what the quest for the historical Jesus has actually achieved in the interpretation of the primitive christian kerygma. Here we must again turn to Bultmann. For in the first place we would agree with him when he brings out the distinction between the historical Jesus and the kerygma of Christ,[45] even if we would have reservations about the way in which he sometimes formulates the distinction.

When Bultmann says that in the kerygma the mythical figure of the Son of God has replaced the historical person of Jesus,[46] it may be merely a somewhat imprecise formulation, which is not intended for instance to deny that when the kerygma speaks of the Son of God it claims to speak of Jesus, by actually predicating this title of him. On the other hand, when we read later the more carefully formulated phrase that the kerygma 'put itself in the place of the historical Jesus',[47] this seems to correspond exactly to what Bultmann is saying in his essay. It may be then that the choice of phrase in the first quotation was not quite so random as we imagined.

We would also have to ask whether the distinction is really

brought out when it is presented as a time-difference in the eschatological history of salvation.[48] Even though the tradition would seem to support such a view, we must try and get behind it by interpreting the two sides of the distinction in the light of their understanding of eschatology. We must ask whether Jesus did not move beyond an apocalyptic understanding of eschatology in a way which corresponds most remarkably to Paul's own treatment of it. For Paul does indeed use apocalyptic ideas, but in such a way that they are transformed by his understanding that in Jesus the decisive eschatological event has already taken place.[49]

I also find it difficult to accept formulations of the distinction which suggest that the kerygma demands that we believe in more things than Jesus demanded.[50] It may be that such questions in the debate with Bultmann are of considerable importance; for at the root of them lies the basic problem with which we are concerned in the discussion of the concept of the kerygma and the quest for the historical Jesus. At first, however, they only seem like side issues against the general background of our agreement to treat the difference between the historical Jesus and the kerygma of Christ with the utmost seriousness.

Now it is Bultmann's opinion that no matter what we may discover about the nature (the What) and the manner (the How) of the historical Jesus, it will be irrelevant for the kerygma of Christ in as far as it goes beyond the affirmation of the mere That of the historicity of Jesus.[51] He finds support for this in Paul and John.[52] He only mentions the Synoptics here in order to confute the charge that they could be used to provide arguments against his position. But I do not think that one can be satisfied with such an explanation if one asks what the motive was behind their origin.[53]

Yet perhaps part of the reason for our disagreement here is a confusion about the meaning of the phrase 'the mere That'.[54] It is clear that Bultmann, in taking his stand on the mere That as opposed to the What and the How, is governed by theological considerations, and this is not simply because it is applied to Jesus, but also because of the way in which this point of view is applied. Of course from the point of view of formal logic the That and the What and the How represent different standpoints. We have only to think of the relation of this distinction to the distinction between *existentia* and *essentia* to see what vast fields of philosophical discussion this opens up. The distinction may be applied to historical study, although it will again of course be in the nature of an abstract distinction. I can only know of the That of an historical phenomenon by knowing something of its What and its How, just as knowing the What and the How of an historical phenomenon implies that I know its That. One can indeed be more interested in the one than the other, but never exclusively in the one or the other. Yet the way in which Bultmann speaks of the mere That is not derived from this historical point of view. It has its roots in the way we speak about God.

If we wish to speak of God's reality concretely, and that means with regard to history, then we can only speak of God's act. So in the That of God (or as one can also say in Bultmann's terminology, in the eschatological event) the different elements are combined; it is an event, it cannot be grasped, it cannot be proved, it can only be communicated by the Word, and it can only be accepted by faith. It is moreover in keeping with the subject that this should correspond to the way in which we speak of existence.[55] Now without going into the whole range of problems which this raises, we can at least make one point. Bultmann allows the legitimate (if we can assume this) theological use of the phrase, the That of the eschatological event, which is predicated of an historical (*geschichtlich*) event, to run over, in my opinion unjustifiably, into a use where the 'That' is applied in a purely historical (*historisch*) sense to the mere facticity of an historical event. For it is neither possible to establish an historical relationship to a mere That, as it were, *in vacuo*, nor is it in accordance with the theological meaning of the That that it should be predicated of an abstract historical fact. Rather the theological intention of talk about the That of God, is that it should be confessed and believed in relation to the What and the How of historic reality.

Now in fact Bultmann's own statements about the historical Jesus serve only to confirm this, if one looks at them in detail. His attempt to find support for the statement 'that one does not *need* to go beyond the That,'[56] by appealing to Paul and John, will scarcely hold water; for they both find that there is a basic minimum of historical 'What and How', no matter how small, which is necessary for the kerygma.[57] The important thing here is not a detailed assessment of the facts. Apart from the crucifixion, the fundamental thing for Bultmann is that Jesus preached.[58] Here again we notice that the What and the How are not completely unimportant by comparison with the pure That. For Bultmann too it is 'a matter of course *that Jesus' preaching was kerygmatic.*'[59] Here, again, there is no question of working this out in detail; trying to see how much we can trace back to Jesus and how much has its roots in early Christianity. Not that these questions of historical detail, and above all the exhaustive interpretation of the Jesuanic tradition, would be unimportant. We must remain open for anything that we could learn from that source, while at the same time we must now go straight to the root of the matter by asking the question: Is it possible to determine the point where the historical Jesus and the primitive christian kerygma converge, in such a way that the difference between the two is not lost from sight, but they can cast light on each other by virtue of their differences?

Bultmann himself gives an answer to this which touches the *nervus rerum*: 'One may well say that the appearance and message of Jesus imply, in so far as he called for a decision with regard to his own person as the bearer of the Word of God, a decision on which depends salvation or rejection. The confession of the community which is given in the kerygma would then have to be understood as the explicit form of response to the call to decision, of the obedience which acknowledges God's revelation in Jesus.'[60] Thus Bultmann defines the relation of Jesus and the primitive christian kerygma in terms of implicit and explicit Christology,[61] or, as we could formulate without distorting his meaning (even if as far as I know he nowhere does this), in terms of implicit christological kerygma and explicit christological kerygma. Now this, as Bultmann himself recognises, makes it 'intelligible for us how the preacher became the one who is preached.'[62] And this is indeed, or so one would have thought, an answer to the question to what extent the kerygma of Christ, the faith in Christ, depends on Jesus himself; indeed it is an answer which shows that the main concern of the appearance of Jesus and the kerygma of Christ is identical. It is, that is to say, an answer which allows us to recognise beyond the mere That of the appearance of Jesus, the true importance of the person of Jesus. It shows us that the What of his appearance is the presupposition of the kerygma of Christ, because it implies it and is in turn made explicit by it.

It is therefore all the more surprising that Bultmann rejects this insight into the relation of Jesus and the primitive christian kerygma as implicit and explicit Christology as basically unimportant, as affecting in no way the supreme importance of the That, of the pure historicity of the historical Jesus. It is by no means easy to understand his reasons for this. 'For to show that the kerygma goes back to the claim of Jesus contained in his work, does not prove the material unity between the work and message of Jesus and the kerygma.'[63] Now what is meant here by material unity if it is not established by the fact that the kerygma made explicit what the ministry and preaching of Jesus and his very person implied? Some explanation seems to be suggested by Bultmann's remark that such observations 'still move within the field of discourse of traditional historical critical enquiry and its categories,'[64] that in this way one can only show the historical continuity between the ministry of Jesus and the kerygma,[65] so that one gets no further than answering the question of 'the causality of the historical event'.[66] Bultmann seems to say that in this way one can indeed establish the relation between the call to decision and the response, but that one cannot show that the response is true. Now of course he is perfectly right in as far as he wants to guard against the illegitimate attempt[67] to by-pass the question of belief by demonstrating certain historical phenomena, i.e. by equating the historical demonstration with the proof of the truth of faith. For the fact that the christological kerygma is the answer to the eschatological call to decision of Jesus demonstrates the truth neither of the call nor of the response. It does not even make one face the challenge presented, and still less does it say anything about the truth of this challenge. We would agree completely with Bultmann that the mere historical observation of an eschatological challenge does not mean that one feels the weight of this challenge oneself.[68] For it is possible to recognise Jesus as an eschatological event, only by making the eschatological self-understanding one's own; and this is not the same as classifying Jesus' self-understanding historically as eschatological.

Now Bultmann is right to guard against such dangers. Yet at the same time we should not lose sight of the fact that historical criticism has not shown that the kerygma is just a particular, perhaps even completely erroneous, answer to Jesus' call to decision. Rather, by going beyond what Bultmann understands by 'continuity', it has shown that it is indeed a wholly appropriate and relevant answer. Primitive Christianity understood Jesus aright, however little Jesus was responsible for the way in which it formulated this understanding.[69] The figure of Jesus does not appear in an arbitrary disguise in the christological kerygma, for the kerygma makes explicit that which was implicit in his person, i.e. in his appearance and preaching. Nor can I see what can be meant by defining this relation in terms of implicit and explicit Christology, unless it be that such historical judgment[70] forces one into asserting the 'material unity of the ministry and preaching of Jesus with the kerygma'.

Yet what is the matter with which we are concerned here? Bultmann asserts that historical enquiry can lead to no more than the observation of an 'historical continuity' and that this is not enough to show the 'material agreement'. Moreover there is a strong connection between this statement and his other view that we can only speak of the 'matter' with which Jesus was concerned in terms of 'That' and not of 'What'. On the one hand it is an expression of the inappropriateness of historical enquiry that it is unable to show[71] the 'material unity of the ministry and preaching of Jesus with the kerygma'; on the other, Bultmann sees it as fully in accordance with the nature of the 'matter' with which we are concerned —a 'matter' where we are concerned not with the 'What' but with the 'That'—that a material unity in terms of the 'What' should be of no relevance whatsoever.

Once again we are confronted with the formula 'the mere That', which is so characteristic of Bultmann's thought. It is significant too that in this instance its relation to the other formula, 'implicit Christology',[72] is strongly stressed. For the 'That' is the 'matter' with which we are concerned here. Or to put it somewhat provocatively in Bultmann's own terminology: the That is the What in which Jesus and the primitive christian kerygma converge. Bultmann himself has shown this That to be the 'material unity of the ministry and proclamation of Jesus with the kerygma'.[73] The confusing thing here is that on the one hand the concept of the That is charged with the greatest possible meaning as the eschatological call to decision—we can now add: of the Word of God—which takes place here and now; on the other hand it is emptied of all meaning as the mere historicity of the person of Jesus. The intention behind this is perfectly clear. An explanation has to be found for the strange fact that a mere repetition of his preaching[74] and a biographical presentation of his personality does not give an adequate 'repetition' of that which is decisive in the appearance of Jesus. Rather the preacher must become the preached in such a way that the 'matter' with which he was concerned becomes explicit through the proclamation of his 'Name' as the Word of God. Yet the confusing thing about Bultmann's interpretation remains that his concentration on the That, although it should actually be seen as an attempt to find an extremely wide theological concept for the Word of God, in fact has the appearance of a formal reduction to the mere fact that the Word comes to pass. Yet all may still be well so long as one holds fast to two considerations; firstly, that for the Word of God the That and the What are identical, and secondly, in what way they are identical. For God's Word does not mean any word, but pure word, pure address, and this means authoritative word,[75] word which creates faith. Its 'content' is completely exhausted by its 'event' (coming to pass) and its 'event' is its 'content' —which can be made explicit!

Bultmann has attempted to emphasise the contrast between his own view and the traditional understanding of the Word. He set his own interpretation of the 'Word of God' as that which constitutes the unity between Jesus and the primitive christian kerygma, against the simple equation with, on the one side, Jesus' words, and on the other, with words reported about Jesus. For just as Jesus as 'event' is the Word of God,[76] so also is the kerygma.[77] But how are the two halves of this comparison linked together? And why is this understanding of the Word of God tied to the name of Jesus? Here we are faced with another task of interpretation which we must carry through—apparently in contradiction to Bultmann—if we are to be true to his intention. On the one side we have to cast light on this understanding of the Word of God by an examination of *the proclamation and activity of Jesus*: on the other hand we have to interpret the kerygma in such a way that we show —as is obviously in accordance with its nature—how its character as Word of God depends on its *invocation of the name of Jesus.*

Now these are insights and tasks which still properly speaking lie within the field of historical enquiry, i.e. of an enquiry which is prepared to enter into the internal structure of the subject matter of which the New Testament texts speak, yet without becoming identical with the decision of faith itself.[78] The problem of interpretation which is posed by the primitive christian kerygma could be put in yet another way. The primitive christian christological kerygma did not come into being because Jesus had already taught Christology. Rather, the christological kerygma arose as an answer to the call to decision made by Jesus,[79] which was given its sharpest form by Jesus' own death. Christological kerygma arose out of a situation qualified by Jesus.[80] As such, the situation which was qualified by Jesus also belongs inseparably to the christological kerygma; for it is this which makes it necessary and legitimate, which is therefore the condition of its understanding and its criterion. For an answer can only be understood as an answer with regard to the word which calls it forth. Where we are concerned with the Word as an event, it is clear that the situation belongs to the Word itself. Whatever claims to make something explicit can only be understood in the light of that in which it is implicit. The exposition does not make the text superfluous, but can only be validated by reference to the text itself. Thus Bultmann's statement that the 'kerygma presupposes the historical Jesus,' that without him there would have been no kerygma,[81] may seem painfully obvious; yet it is of the utmost importance, for it is constitutive for the understanding of the kerygma. For Christology is not grounded in Christ because he gave rise to the primitive christian Christology by himself teaching Christology; it arose as a result of the authority with which he gave concrete utterance to God, and thereby was able to qualify the situation in such a way that the question of faith or unfaith became acute. No understanding of the primitive christian kerygma is possible without taking into account the way in which Jesus thus qualified and illumined the situation in which he spoke.[82]

We have been led to these views by our reflections on the question of the historical Jesus and its importance for the understanding of the primitive christian kerygma; this in turn sprang out of our consideration of the concept of kerygma which first caused us to enquire into the question of the historical Jesus.[83] It is now time to consider the importance of these views for systematic theology[84] and this in particular with regard to the concept of the kerygma. For merely to enumerate the conditions for understanding the primitive christian kerygma is not immediately to give an answer to the question how we are to understand the kerygma as kerygma today—a question which can be put in another way: how we are to proclaim kerygma as kerygma today?

We cannot avoid the seriousness of this question. There was a time when men were less aware of this; for some reason they saw the christological kerygma in such a way that faith became a law imposed on their situation. In recent years, as W. Herrmann rightly saw, the question of the ground of faith has become the most burning theological problem of all, for it is a question which touches the roots of our preaching.[85] This means in other words that the Word of God itself has been put in question. Of what nature is the word-event which we speak of as the Word of God, what answer does it give to, and how does it shed light on the question of the intelligibility, the credibility, the pertinence, the authority, of speech about God? It may indeed seem strange that this question is still being asked, that it is in fact being asked with more urgency than ever before, when for forty years theology has stood under the banner of the rediscovered concept of the Word of God. Yet these years have taught us that we must not allow this theology to degenerate into a mere epoch of theological restoration. Rather we must again attempt to discover the fundamental meaning of the Word of God. We have to think again what we mean by 'God' when we say 'the Word of God', and we have to do this by reflecting on the event-character of the Word, or alternatively on the word-character of the event, in which God comes to expression, in which God makes himself understood.

Bultmann rejected the quest for the historical Jesus as being irrelevant for faith, in order to bring out clearly the nature of the Word of God. Now in this he was right, in so far as the quest for the historical Jesus was intended to afford an historical proof which would do away with faith and make us independent of the Word. Yet it seems to me that we can only justify the theology of the Word of God by taking up the quest for the historical Jesus in the right way. For what is it that makes out of the kerygma the word-event in which God is no longer an unintelligible cipher, but is also present as the one who makes our reality real? Thus if the question of the historical Jesus is to help us here, it will not be by seeking to get behind the Word of proclamation, but on the contrary, by penetrating further into the Word. Such an enquiry is made, not to avoid the challenge of the Word of God, but so that one can truly hear the challenge and understand the kerygma as the Word of God.

But how can the quest for the historical Jesus help us here? Certainly not by giving a mere 'repetition' of Jesus' proclamation,[86] which would no more help than would the mere repetition of the primitive christian kerygma. Here Bultmann would of course agree. Yet he does not explain why it is that the christological kerygma, which is also in the first place an historical phenomenon, can be 'repeated' in the true sense of the word, that is to say can be proclaimed today, while he denies this to be true of the challenge and call of Jesus.[87] He is content to point to the self-understanding of the primitive christian kerygma as eschatological event. Yet he does not ask the question which he asks of the eschatological consciousness of Jesus, i.e. how the kerygma of Christ can be handed on as eschatological event without being reduced to a mere historical phenomenon, but being handed on in such a way that it reveals the eschatological self-understanding and that means faith.

Now Bultmann of course sees that the eschatological authority of the christian kerygma, in so far as it really exists and can be handed on, is connected with the invocation of Jesus. Now if the invocation of Jesus is seen as an invocation of the mere That, then it does no more than give expression to the claim of the kerygma itself. For the kerygma claims that Christ is present in it, in that the kerygma 'has taken the place of the historical Jesus'.[88] Thus the difference between the christological kerygma and Jesus is eliminated with a vengeance. The invocation of Jesus merely retains the character of a paradoxical eschatological call to faith. It is impossible to interpret it to show in what way it is the source of authority and the ground of faith which is here named.[89] If the difference between the kerygma of Christ and the historical Jesus disappears, we shall not only have to fear that the church may usurp the position of the historical Jesus,[90] we shall also have to ask whether in the end, in spite of the assertion of the real presence of Christ in the kerygma,[91] it may not rather be the case that the kerygma has taken the place of something which is absent.[92]

If there *can* be kerygma today as kerygma, then it is because it is *necessary*, and that means because the situation is qualified kerygmatically. Now it is true that this kerygmatic qualification of the situation is the business of the kerygma itself, but here we must make two reservations: firstly, that the proclamation must deal with the actual situation, in order to bring its true reality to expression; secondly, that the proclamation must not be reduced to explicit christological kerygma. For this has been shown by our reflections on the relation of the historical Jesus and the primitive christian kerygma. Explicit christological kerygma has its basis in implicit christological kerygma, that is in the person of Jesus himself. Explicit christological kerygma is derived from the fact that Jesus gave concrete expression to God. This is what the kerygma confesses; it is the sum of all christological predications: Jesus—the Word of God. In him God came. Jesus has made God intelligible. Our task is to see what light the fact of Jesus' priority over the christological kerygma and of his difference from it can shed on the intelligibility and meaningfulness of the kerygma. Even the kerygma finds it important to retain the situation out of which it arose, by retaining the name of Jesus. This name—and by this we mean that which has come to expression in Jesus—is the basis of the christological kerygma. It is true of course that the christological kerygma cannot be made intelligible as kerygma today simply by historical interpretation. Just as it would be wrong to suppose that the christological kerygma is intelligible in itself. Christological kerygma can only be understood as kerygma in a kerygmatically qualified situation. So we find that what we had seen to be historically true now has general validity.

This kerygmatic qualification is identical with implicit Christology. It would be wrong to suppose that as soon as we have explicit Christology we no longer need implicit Christology. This would indeed be true if we were only interested in expounding a set of ideas. But 'implicit' Christology is not concerned with concealed christological ideas but with an event which claims men's obedience. It is concerned with a situation which is qualified by the challenge to Christology, by the permission of Christology. It is this event alone, and not the authority of any ideas which the kerygma may have made its own, which legitimates the homological form of explicit Christology. Explicit Christology, which exists in its own right, threatens to conceal and forget its true ground, and so to lose its footing and support. Instead of implicit Christology being made superfluous by explicit Christology, it becomes all the more important. For the sake of the kerygma as kerygma we must listen to the implicit christological kerygma behind the explicit christological kerygma. This is to say that the really important thing is the speech about God which qualifies the kerygmatic situation as such, which shows the situation in its true light. Speaking about God is a condition of the understanding of Christology only if it has the character of implicit Christology. If we are not confronted with implicit christological kerygma, explicit christological kerygma remains utterly void, without authority, without reality. Implicit christological kerygma is that word-event in which the encounter with Jesus brings God to expression in the reality in which we live. It is that word-event where God is brought to expression in such a way that this confrontation leads to the basis of faith, that is to say that it becomes the event which establishes our faith. Only then can christological predications receive any meaning.

Encounter with the man Jesus means encounter with him who came to expression in him. Here there are three factors involved: the texts which have brought him to expression; the present day witnesses who bring him to expression as a result of listening to the texts; and our fellow men among whom we live, in whom he brings himself to expression.

Now if we can say of the man Jesus that through him God comes to expression in such a way that we come to know Jesus himself as the Word which brings certainty and therefore as the point where reality is radically challenged; if this is so, then we have the clearest indication of how it is that the kerygma, as the homology of certainty, finds its support in Jesus.

Now if Jesus is known as the Word[93] which brings certainty, this means that we come to know him as the Gospel and the basis of faith. The fact that Jesus brings certainty also involves him *eo ipso* in a relation to the law. For in that he becomes the basis of faith, in that he is the Gospel with which we are confronted, giving us certainty of salvation, he meets us in our own situation, in uncertainty which is the essence of sin. Jesus verifies the reality which confronts us. He makes us certain of our relation to it. He shows us the law into whose power we have fallen, in its true light. For part of man's dilemma is his confusion with regard to the law to which he is subjected. We are to come to know Jesus as the Word which makes us certain; but this will only bring us certainty of our salvation as freedom from the law—i.e. it will only give us the Gospel—if we at the same time come to a clear knowledge of the reality which confronts us, by becoming acquainted with an *interpretatio legis* which condemns and takes hold of our conscience. We can only speak of the certainty of faith through the Gospel which sets our conscience free, in the same breath as we speak of the certainty of the law which condemns our conscience (i.e. the certainty of sin). It is for this reason that in our search for the situation in which the christological kerygma can be understood, we shall have to concentrate on the encounter with the man Jesus who became subject to the law in order to free its subjects. If we did not encounter in Jesus both the law and the Gospel alongside each other, if we did not encounter him as the Word which brings a double certainty, then at best we could see the christological kerygma as a mythological description of a gift which leads us into the realms of fantasy; we could scarcely see it as a hymn of faith to the God who seeks us out in this our reality, who lets himself be found in this reality, and who thus offers us his salvation from the cross in the word of life in repentance.

The difficulty of preaching today leads us to the fact that man has so far fallen victim to the law that he no longer even has any idea of it. How should certainty of salvation have any meaning for him, if he is not certain of the law to which he is subject? This is the real core of our theological task. How can we find the basis of a Word, no matter how modest, which is certain and which brings certainty? What is it that can assert an unconditional authority over men today, including of course ourselves? It is essential that we should follow the urgent dictates of conscience as a guide for the proper interpretation of theology. This is to be true to Jesus whom we confess as Lord. If Jesus encounters us as the Word which brings certainty, then the truly remarkable thing about this, which can be neither replaced nor superseded by anything else, is that by distinguishing between the law and the Gospel he gives certainty for the certain distinction between God and man.

IV

Towards a Christology

1. Christology interprets the homology: 'I believe in Jesus.' All forms of confession of Christ, even when they are not expressly preceded by the formula 'I believe', are variations on the homology, 'I believe in Jesus'. Christological formulae predicated of Jesus (titles and kerygmatic statements) serve to make faith in Jesus explicit. They make an explicit 'I believe' unnecessary, because it is already implied by the homological forms of the language itself. Thus the fundamental hermeneutic rule for Christology is to interpret faith in Jesus homologically. Thus christological predications and titles must be traced back to the homology, 'I believe in Jesus', which they make explicit. Further, this basic homology must be interpreted as a homological *event*. So Christology must reflect on the homological *situation* of faith, in order to bring to expression the necessity which faith makes possible, and which allows faith to find its proper expression in homologies.

2. The measure of a properly conducted Christology (*die Sachlichkeit der Christologie*) is whether it acts as the advocate (*Sachwalterin*) of the word-event from which faith draws sustenance and which it brings to expression homologically. The cause (*Sache*) of Christology *is* not the homology. Rather the homology is the consequence of the 'cause' of Christology. Thus by throwing light on the real nature of the homology we also throw light on the real nature of the cause of Christology. The cause of Christology is homological, i.e. it finds its appropriate counterpart in the linguistic

structure of faith. The language of homology is the language of consent. This means that the community of thought and speech, i.e. unanimity with what others have said and do say, is a not unimportant but necessarily secondary 'moment' in the structure. Such agreement however does not make an homology an homology. Rather it presupposes homology and demands that our consent be given only homologically. The fact of the matter (*Sachver halt*) concerning the language of consent is essentially this: by joining myself to a Word which 'speaks to me', I become myself by being confronted by a tribunal of enquiry; this leads me to demand of others the same consent in order to put an end to the questioning. Thus in the homology there are three moments which are intimately related to one another: that I should identify myself with a Word that identifies me; that this identification with a Word *extra me* should compel me to take responsibility for it; and that such a language of consent should call others to consent.

3. Homology means speaking with certainty. It is speech which is concerned with life itself, as it is lived out in its encounters, with life which one must therefore be prepared to answer for. We can best grasp the essence of homology by allowing our thoughts to be directed towards the 'event' of that which makes the homology necessary. Although there can be various modes of homological speech (testimonies in court, confessions of love, statements of opinion, confessions of faith), each of which betrays much the same language structure, we are not so much concerned with analysing the formal structures, as with the question: what is the ground of the basic necessity of homology? There is the most intimate agreement between the statement that homology is concerned with life itself and the statement that by throwing light on the real nature of homology, we also throw light on the real nature of the subject of Christology.

4. If the cause of Christology which comes to expression in the homology, 'I believe in Jesus', has to be interpreted as a homo-

logical 'event', then we should start with the question: how far does *Jesus* arouse faith as agreement with him, and that is to say as courage to associate oneself with his words (*Einstimmen*)? If this is not merely a matter of partial interest, but one which concerns the whole of life, that is to say if this is a decision which affects one's own humanity, then we can state the matter as follows. The Word is Jesus himself, showing himself as the Word of life which brings certainty, i.e. as the Word which calls us to the encounter with himself, which makes our own speech possible.

5. To say that agreement (*Einverständnis*) with Jesus shows itself homologically as *belief* in him means this: Jesus encounters us as the pure Word of promise which identifies man by virtue of what is promised to him as the future (new) man, and with regard to his present state as the past (old) man. So joining in with Jesus means identifying *myself* with the Word which *he* is, in such a way that I can regard that which I am as already the past man, because I entrust myself to the future which is promised to me as one who has already embarked on this future life. For this reason faith which invokes Jesus is certainty and life, yet not in the normal sense of these words; for it is found in the encounter with that which is encountered only in the Word, which can thus come to expression only in the language of faith, i.e. in homology.

6. Agreement with Jesus, and that means faith seen as entrusting oneself to the pure Word of promise, is *as such* invocation of *God*. Nor can we deduce the fact that to speak of agreement with Jesus is necessarily to speak of God, merely from the historical fact that Jesus himself talked about God. For one can neither receive historical information about God, nor can one speak historically about God; one can only speak about him homologically. Nor should one attempt to introduce any preconceived idea about God into the discussion in the hope that it may serve to give some explanation of what one is about. Jesus, the Word which frees men's consciences for faith and for love, overcomes all idols and concepts of God at

the same time as he disarms the radical uncertainty or indifference which holds the godless in thrall. The occurrence of this event which overthrows the powers of this world, which is the verification and fulfilment of man's consciousness that he is called by some unconditional authority, can only be expressed as the intervention of God himself, as the occasion of his coming. For the confidence and certainty of faith is something radically different from man's self-assurance; it means that I seek the ground of my certainty *extra me*; it means the certainty and confidence in God which is first offered to us by Jesus. For he shows us that we may share in the omnipotence of God, that we are called by God's Word and are ourselves empowered to call on God himself. The necessity which makes such speech about God possible is grounded in the fact that our consent to Jesus is not a partial homological occurrence but is homological existence because it reveals man in the revelation of God.

7. The question of certainty is man's basic question, because it is identical with human being as being that is questioned. As such it is often distorted and disguised by man's own determined efforts to dispose of it. Thus there can be no neutral analysis of the question of certainty. Yet one's conscious or unconscious approach to the analysis of the question of certainty must prove itself with reference to the many different ways in which the question of certainty is experienced. This also holds true of theology in particular, which raises the question of certainty in the radical sense as a theme, starting from the certainty of faith.

8. The actual question about certainty can never be answered by turning it into a question which can be answered from one's knowledge of objectively determined facts. In such a question it becomes evident that we are concerned with self-assurance. For the attempt to achieve assurance with regard to facts, the attempt to gain control over whatever lies in our power, is no more than a concealed attempt to buttress our self-assurance with achieved

results. Self-assured man feels himself challenged by anything that lies outside his control. Yet this uncertainty with regard to this or that fact only serves to conceal his uncertainty about himself and misleads him into thinking that he can gain security merely by extending his control.

9. The question of certainty is raised in crucial form with regard to the future. For the future is utterly uncertain and as such induces uncertainty, thus leading one to believe that certainty can only be achieved by gaining control over future events. But to locate the question of uncertainty here is misleading. For strictly speaking it is not the events which man seeks to determine which are uncertain; rather it is man who is uncertain with regard to them. He must be assured that the future is constant and determinable, so that it can become the very source of certainty for him. Similarly, what is uncertain about the future is not the future events themselves, but the present state of the man who waits for these events (in so far as they are beyond his control). We can see clearly enough where the root of uncertainty lies if we look at death, which is the one future event about which there is no doubt, but which can nevertheless in no way be said to make a man certain about the future. Nor is this simply because, as the saying goes, what comes after death is unknown and uncontrollable, or because one does not even know if there is anything after death; this would merely be to turn the sting of death into a question of incomplete knowledge. In such a view, death would not be death if it were not the end of our ability to control and determine things. Yet it is not only in death that we are confronted by things we cannot determine or control, however true this is also of death. The root of uncertainty does not lie in things which we are unable to determine or control, but in the indeterminability, uncontrollability and questionableness of man himself. To be more precise the true root of uncertainty lies in the fact that man feels the uncertainty of his own inability to determine and control himself. In the most profound sense uncertainty is

man's unwillingness to face up to the truth about himself, is his disunity with himself, is the lie about his own existence. Uncertainty is of the very nature of sin, which is, in Paul's words, the sting of death.

10. The question of certainty has its seat in the conscience. This is suggested by the relation between uncertainty and sin. But the nature of this relation becomes problematic if we ask whether uncertainty is the *cause* of sin, as a result of the conscience failing to give instructions, or at least to give adequate instructions; or whether uncertainty is not rather the *consequence* of sin, for a bad conscience makes the heart fearful and uncertain (cf. Lev. 26.36). Yet both these questions rest on a false conception of conscience. If we see the root of uncertainty in the conscience's failure to give proper instructions, we assume that the conscience is no more than an ascertainable code of behaviour. If we speak of our bad conscience making us uncertain, it means we have not seen deeply enough, that we have not realised that the conscience which speaks to us is itself man's uncertainty, showing the contradiction of man's being. It is then, so it would seem, but the reverse side of man's rational and free nature, which distinguishes him from the animals. The fact that an animal cannot be uncertain or certain, that it cannot be free or unfree (i.e. that it can neither be untrue to itself nor fulfil itself), that it has neither reason, nor language, nor conscience, that it neither has or does not have time, all these are but aspects of the same matter. Yet we are not concerned with gaining certainty with regard to this or that thing by the use of our reason and freedom, but with being empowered to use our reason and freedom by a certainty which determines the person of man himself. The very fact that the *question* of certainty is so acute, is a sign of the uncertainty of man's being. Nor do we have any other experience of man than this. But the fact that man does feel in this way about himself is precisely the proof that man who is uncertain is at odds with himself.

11. Now we can gain an idea of existential certainty from the partial experience of it which we do in fact enjoy. When a man acknowledges his guilt, when he is comforted in a hopeless situation, when he accedes to the enormous demands which are made of him at a particular moment, or quite simply when he is happy, when he is completely engrossed in something, when he is deeply in love, when he is firmly set on some course of action, he does gain some knowledge of certainty. The man who is certain is clearly at one with himself, he is, that is to say, truly rational and free. We can only define certainty by pointing to various situations in which man finds himself. For certainty is a question of time. Uncertain man is unsettled and divided by time, whether it be in his relation to the past (e.g. boasting), or to the future (e.g. worry), or to the thing which is present but not timely (e.g. his distraction, lack of concentration). In all this he is divided among himself, he is out of harmony with time. The man who is certain, on the other hand, is the man who is contemporaneous with himself (that is the true meaning of Kierkegaard's[1] concept of contemporaneousness). He knows and does what is timely. Thus we experience certainty most often in unambiguous situations which make their claims on us clearly and forcibly, while uncertainty is most virulent as we gain insight into ourselves in those moments of present indecision which leave us speechless (in despair, fear and boredom). Yet such experience of certainty is only partial: firstly because it is limited to particular situations which make particular demands on us and only give us a particular kind of certainty. Again, because it only brings certainty within this defined field which thus limits us in the way we can communicate it to others. Thirdly, because it is not adequate to deal with the basic uncertainty which is the root of all uncertainty. For even successful works cannot make the conscience certain.

12. The interrelated ways in which certainty can be—partially—imparted are these: the experience of concrete situations, teaching

and—which is indeed the most powerful of all the ways in which a man can influence another—example. Jesus exerts incomparable power through the combined effect of his words and actions. He will not leave us alone, because we can neither free ourselves from the question of certainty nor from the impression which he gives us of *what* certainty is, and that there is such a thing as certainty. Christian faith can be seriously accepted as faith in *Jesus* only where we properly accept Jesus himself as example. The idea of the imitation of Jesus' example has only become suspect because it has so often been very superficially understood. Yet the suspicion of Jesus' example has in turn led to the relation of faith to Jesus becoming abstract. Of course one can never do justice to a man's example merely by imitating certain outward forms of his behaviour; it can only be achieved by conforming to his behaviour, by allowing oneself to be encouraged to corresponding certainty. Yet even here the effect of the example is restricted to the realisation of partial certainty in particular actions, and is consequently limited to analogous situations. Yet the power with which the figure of Jesus speaks to us questions even our relation to him as an example. For here we are confronted by certainty which, because it determines *all* behaviour, because it relates to *every* situation, because it is not partial certainty, permits no *analogous* realisation, but spurs us on to allow ourselves to be drawn into *this* certainty. Yet our relation to Jesus as our example is still not without effect precisely because it is itself questionable; for the fact that we cannot achieve a certainty analogous to that of Jesus means that the question of our own certainty can be put in its most radical form.

13. The certainty of Jesus is neither a partial aspect of his appearance, nor is it merely related to a part of reality; it is of the very nature of his person. This is the mystery of his person which the traditional dogmatic notion of his perfect sinlessness points to (even if it lends itself too easily to moralistic misconceptions). The concrete forms of this certainty are these: *freedom*, in which man

is no longer unsettled by the past and the future, but which allows him to be present to do and say what is timely; *authority*, which necessarily follows from this freedom; *love*, which is made possible for us by our freedom. Such fundamental certainty is not only relevant to exceptional situations, but has its place in everyday human life because it is directed to man in his basic uncertainty and can therefore be called out by any situation; for it lives on that which lies hidden in every situation. Jesus' life was an existence based on this kind of certainty. As such his energy was not exhausted by his efforts to achieve security for himself, and so he was free to give himself for all who stand in need of the certainty which makes us certain; indeed he was able to give himself in such a way that his death was not the end but the fulfilment of his life for others. Thus Jesus acts as man's representative; he is certain for others and in their stead, lest they should be abandoned to uncertainty; he opens the way for them into the life of certainty. But to be men's representative by virtue of his certainty and to lead them into certainty means no less than to be God's representative. For to live contemporaneously with oneself, to avoid both the way of the legalist whose existence is bound to the past, and the way of the apocalyptist whose existence is rigidly tied to the future, to live, that is, in the present, *is* the existence in fulfilled time, eschatological existence, life in the presence of God. It is not the life of an animal, which has no knowledge of today or tomorrow; nor is it the life of the self-assured man who seeks to draw the sting of the past and the future by his own toughness (and only succeeds in making it all the stronger): but it is the life of man in temptation, who clings not to the past but to God as his true origin; who clings not to future events but to God as the true future, who enters into the present, which is the present of the Eternal One, the experience both of abandonment by God and of certainty in God. Jesus' certainty only receives its fulness because it is rooted in the present by virtue of his assent to the nearness of the Father to the Son, a nearness which is all-embracing, which we cannot ourselves control; only so is the nearness of the Father credible, only so can it bring certainty. Such certainty in God represents God himself by promising God to man and so passing judgment on all substitutes for God.

14. Existence in fundamental certainty does not exist for its own benefit, but bears fruit as the certainty which brings certainty, i.e. by freeing man for an existence in certainty. Faith which is certainty in God, because it partakes in God's omnipotence, is faith which produces faith. Yet being set free to believe is the opposite of fascination. So the certainty which brings certainty is not only accompanied by the sign of authority but also by the appearance of powerlessness. Wherever faith is aroused, unfaith is also set on its guard. The existence in certainty is certain of the cross, because the existence in uncertainty will attempt to secure itself by becoming entrenched in its own legalistic piety. Thus it is one of the facts about Jesus that from time to time he may have many fellow-travellers, but that in reality he has few disciples. Yet his work of bringing certainty to men was completed when he died abandoned by God and men. Now we may be tempted to misconstrue the fact that, seemingly, Jesus himself aroused only little faith—and that very weak—until after his death. We may say that what Jesus was unable to achieve, was furnished by the additional fact of his resurrection, as if the post-resurrection faith was something other than the consequence of Jesus' certainty. But this would be to turn away from the certainty of faith of the historical Jesus and to stray into the realms of pseudo-historical certainty, of a self-certainty based on mythology. We will find the key to a proper understanding of this only when we see that the death of Jesus in relation to his certainty which makes us certain, is not a chance accident but a necessity for salvation, is, in fact, *the* salvation event itself. Now we must not see this as a sort of satisfaction theory, where God allows himself to be reconciled, to have his mind changed by the sacrifice which is offered—for this would make Jesus the witness of unfaith! Rather

Jesus' death is necessary because in his self-giving certainty God shows himself to men as self-giving, reconciling love; shows himself, not as a vague concept but as the utterable Word, and thus makes faith, i.e. consent, possible for all.

15. Jesus' certainty in God was able in its temporal form to arouse faith on particular occasions, i.e. to bring certainty to lead men into his contemporaneousness. Yet this always had the limitation that the fulfilled time would be confused with a particular stage of history, that faith would be mistaken for eyewitness, that the Word which brings certainty would be confused with a type of enthusiastic apocalyptic experience. That is to say, the temporal presence of Jesus concealed the radical eschatological character of his certainty, because it restricted the situation of faith (chronologically speaking) to chance meetings with Jesus and did not yet reveal faith as eschatological existence for all the world. The *verbum dei incarnatum* gains a hearing, and that means achieves its goal as the *verbum Dei*, only when it is known as the *verbum dei predicatum*. Jesus places us radically in the situation of faith only when he addresses us as the crucified, i.e. as the one who is no longer present. In this way through his Word which occurs here and now, he opens up his eschatological existence for *everyone* in *his* situation. The proclamation of Jesus' certainty after his death, together with the consenting and accepting reply of faith, came to expression as the raising of Jesus, because in it the life of Jesus was manifested. Now while this was in some way to borrow from apocalyptic thought, at the same time it burst the bonds of the apocalyptic by showing Jesus as the present eschaton. Now this is not to destroy time but rather it means that man must no longer await the future with uncertainty, but can accept it in faith as the fulfilled time. The proclamation of the eschatological resurrection in the person of one particular individual is unusual from the point of view of comparative religion, but it corresponds to the certainty of God in the present which was manifested in Jesus. And the only

faith which can correspond to that kerygma is the participation in the certainty of God in the present.

16. The proclamation based on Jesus, which invokes him as the salvation of the world, proclaims, as the one thing necessary, that faith which is certainty of existence, which is a conscience freed from guilt and fear, a foundation *extra se*, an establishment *supra legem*, unity with oneself, all this because man is reconciled with God. The problem of Christology is seen then most sharply as the problem whether faith, if we take its necessity for granted, remains rooted in Jesus, and in what way it can be seen as faith in Jesus. Thus anyone who seeks to separate faith as certainty from Jesus, will not only have to see where this leads him, but also have to say what he understands by certainty; to see whether he can *proclaim* faith and to say what he thinks of Jesus. To reduce the question of the relation of faith to Jesus to a mere question in the history of ideas, would be to fail to understand the problem of the basis of faith, to fail to see that man in his uncertainty can never achieve certainty unless he is confronted by it. Certainty confronts a man, when that which concerns him ultimately[2] becomes that which he willingly affirms; it confronts him when his predicament becomes full of promise, when his inability to control his own destiny becomes the gift of his freedom, when his death becomes the arrival of life, his time the place of eternity. An integral part of the event of such certainty is the conjunction of compulsion and freedom, law and grace. Now of course human life is continually full to the brim with both. As such, any time is an occasion for certainty, and any uncertainty is sin. Yet one comes to know certainty only as one comes to know the distinction which man in his uncertainty cannot make: namely between *tempus legis* and *tempus gratiae*[3], between *homo peccator* and *Deus justificans*.[4]

V

Towards an ecclesiology

1. The confusing and contradictory collection of bodies which claim for themselves the title of 'church' all agree on one point: their identity with that which made its appearance in primitive Christianity as the *ekklesia*. This is the starting point for any attempt to say what the church is. As soon as we look at its history we are immediately confronted with imprecision, tensions and disputes. Yet we may discern one characteristic which is constitutive for the church. The decisive thing is the authoritative word-event with its invocation of Jesus, which unites Jews and Gentiles. It unites them in allowing God to be present as the enabler of faith, of the freedom to love and in allowing them to share responsibility for the authoritative word-event in the invocation of Jesus.

2. It is not possible to draw a distinction between the formal definition of the nature of the church and the cause which it is concerned to advocate (comparable to the distinction between the constitution and the aim of a society); rather the church is the event of its basis[1] (cf. Paul's understanding of marriage or the body). It is not enough then merely to insist that the church is concerned solely with Christ, with the Gospel or with faith. We must rather attempt to see how it is that the church which it invokes Christ (or the Gospel or faith) is itself the event of the very thing which invokes. Thus, in laying the foundation of ecclesiology the decisive thing will be to conceive the unity of the content of christian proclamation in such a way that not only are the different *loci* of traditional dog-

matics (theology, Christology, pneumatology, soteriology, eschatology) shown as a single Word, but also that we can show that *what* the Word says is at one with the fact *that* it happens as Word. The point where all these aspects of theology meet is the authority of the presence of God. This is the authority to preach the Word, which, in that it frees man to preach the Word, is also man's authorisation by the Word. Thus the nature of the church lies in the 'word-event', in the reality of its authority and freedom, where authority is understood as freedom and freedom as authority. All ecclesiological statements are thus subject to the criterion of freedom (where freedom is seen as authoritative freedom, i.e. freedom to set free by virtue of the freedom one has oneself received). All the characteristics of the church, as e.g. the breaking down of the divisions between Jews and Gentiles (the prototype of religious particularity) or of the division between pure and impure (the root of the cultic understanding of reality) are an expression of that freedom which has been granted by Jesus Christ.

3. The question of the basis of the church is both closely bound up with, and also carefully to be distinguished from, the question of its historical origins. The church first makes its appearance with the faith which invokes the Risen Jesus and proclaims him as the way to faith for all. Yet this originating 'event', which has been condensed in the tradition by the formation of legends, and split up in the Lucan chronology into the theological schema: Easter, Ascension and Whitsun, has first to undergo a process of clarification with regard to ecclesiology, as is shown by the dispute about the mission to the Gentiles and about the Law. Yet the decisions which were taken on this occasion provided no guarantee that they would be correctly understood, nor indeed that there would be no further confusions. It contradicts the nature of the church to single out any one particular stage of its historical development as a normative pattern for all time. If the church is to remain the church, and that means if it is constantly to be renewed, we shall have to do more

than merely recall its historical originating 'event'. The ground of the church is not present simply because one calls to mind the outpouring of the Spirit at Whitsun (to speak in terms of the Lucan schema), but because of the proclamation of faith which brings with it the promise of the Holy Spirit. The basis of the church is not its beginning, but the authorisation which alone from the beginning was and is the church. The basis of the church, i.e. that which makes the church the church, is not the church itself; in just the same way as it is impossible for the basis of the church to exist without the church, and for the church to exist without its basis.

4. The church itself confesses Jesus as its basis, as is clearly shown by the supreme importance of the invocation of his name. Because the church itself exists as the authoritative 'word-event', its invocation of Jesus designates the basis of its authority. Thus the basis of the church is not something which we can tacitly assume to be present. Only if it is brought out and mentioned by name does it become constitutive for the continuance of the church. Yet the church can hardly invoke its basis simply by pointing to the fact that Jesus founded the church and delegated authority to it by virtue of his own authority. In order to appeal to the delegation of authority as a proof of one's own authority, one must first be able to assume the existence of a recognised authority capable of such delegation. Yet the church cannot simply assume the authority of Jesus; rather it is its task to establish this authority. The authority of the 'word-event' which constitutes the church itself is therefore on the one hand the authority which is felt and established in the word-event itself; yet on the other hand it is the authority which, in accordance with the invocation of Jesus, stems not from the word-event itself but from Jesus. It is the authority of Jesus which is established in the authoritative word-event. Thus it would be a complete contradiction of the structure of this authority if one were to imagine that the church could be legitimated by a specific act of establishment by Jesus, and so to try and discover any statements which Jesus may

have made about establishment and ordering of the church. For the church is not brought into being as a result of certain commands, but through the liberating freedom which authorises man to preach the Word of authority and power.

5. Although traditions about Jesus show a tendency to import post-resurrection events and understanding into the words and attitude of Jesus himself, it is nevertheless remarkable to see how strongly the memory was preserved that the church was not *instituted* during the life of Jesus, and that Jesus did not belong to the early stages of the church (like the founder of a movement or the instigator and organiser of a party). Rather the church was, so to speak, *set free*, by virtue of Jesus' death, as the body, i.e. as the historical presence, of the Risen Lord, in such a way that Jesus both stands over and against the church and is also inseparable from it (which is the relation intended by the expression 'basis' of the church). The rise of faith as men found they were able to preach Jesus, the communication of the spirit as freedom and authority to preach the Word, the institution of baptism in the name of Jesus, which led to the formation of actual communities—all this is placed by tradition quite firmly after Jesus' death as the work of the Risen Lord. The various passages which have been taken as indicating an explicit foundation of the church by Jesus himself, viz. the call and sending out of the twelve, the saying about the keys to Simon Peter, and the institution of the Last Supper, will not stand the test of historical examination. Of course Jesus called disciples, but he did not institute the twelve; Mt. 16 18*f* is, in spite of the underlying Aramaic form, a post-resurrection saying; the command: 'Do this in remembrance of me' is not part of the original words at the Last Supper. Of course this is not to say that Jesus' proclamation of the kingdom of God is as such incompatible with the rise of the church (cf. A. Loisy's dictum: 'Jesus proclaimed the kingdom of God, and what actually came was the church'[2]). On the other hand, the question how far Jesus, although he did not found the church

(in the sense that is of his activity being directed towards that end), is nevertheless the basis of the church, cannot simply be avoided by pointing out (seemingly in accordance with the tradition) that the church had its origins, not in the historical Jesus but in the post-resurrection Christ. For this distinction stands in need of interpretation, the criterion for which is the historical Jesus himself. If the invocation of Jesus is to be at all meaningful, then the ecclesiological relevance of the Easter event is to be seen, not in the fact that it produced the basis of the church, but that it proclaimed the basis and thus distinguished the church from its basis. The revelation of Jesus and the rise of the church, precisely because they are the 'event' of this distinction, are indivisibly one. Thus it follows that the appearance of Jesus himself must be intelligible as implicit ecclesiology.

6. The appearance of Jesus makes its fullest impact on us in the impression of his authority and in the question it raises about the nature of his authority. He was without any authority in the form of a recognisable office or charisma. So the problem and understanding of authority is raised in a radically new form with regard to Jesus. The very diverse expressions of his authority: his teaching, casting out demons, forgiveness of sins, his freedom from legalism and his call to discipleship, have at least this in common, that by setting men free they assert the nearness of God through their *exousia* of the Word. Authority is not simply a concomitant of a certain body of doctrine which can be handed on in the tradition nor is it an independent factor alongside that about which we speak; it is the completed (i.e. not empty) 'word-event' which achieves its purpose (i.e. finds its mark), by leaving God to take care of the future as his province, and so opens up the present to man as freedom to do that which is the pure Word, because it is the presence of God which brings men freedom. Such authority lies essentially beyond our control. We can however bear witness to its exercise, whenever it has occurred, and we can see its exercise as

the authority which brings authority and the freedom which brings freedom. Authority occurs in a personal way in the completed word-event, which distinguishes between God and man by bringing them into conjunction with each other; yet it occurs in such a way that the person in authority demands nothing for himself, but sees only the mission he has received, sees only that he has received authority to serve with authority. The authority which Jesus manifested in his person is shown most clearly in the fact that while Jesus himself assumed the position which had been occupied by the Torah, he did not assume the role of a new lawgiver for the distant God, but proclaimed instead the nearness of God, that men might be free for faith and love. Jesus—and this points to an implicit ecclesiology—looked forward to the day when such authority would bear fruit, yet this could only come to pass if he remained true to his own understanding of authority even in the most extreme weakness.

7. Jesus as the occurrence of authority, as the Gospel in person, is the basis of the church. The church which has issued out of his authority is the continuing presence of that authority. The church which invokes him by calling on his name is endowed with an authority which is only *its own* authority in so far as it remains the authority *of Jesus*. In the problem of authority we find the concurrence of apparently quite disparate aspects of the problem, viz. the question of the historical Jesus, the question of the faith in Christ as the content of the post-resurrection Gospel, and the question of church law, which, when we really think it out, is the question of the right of the church, i.e. of its authority and freedom. *The right of the church consists in bearing witness to the right of Jesus.* (Cf. two of Luther's fundamental assertions about church law: 'Suffer, suffer, cross, cross: that and no other is the right of the Christian.'[3] 'We do indeed have the *ius verbi* but not the *executionem*.'[4] So the church shares the same basic characteristics as the authority of Jesus. It has nothing but the Word; its recognition of the liberating authority of the Word has the character of serving

submission—just as Jesus' dying was the fulfilment of his authority. By virtue of its freedom from the law, it is sent to all men—just as Jesus' authority did not prevent him from going about with sinners. In the certainty of the nearness of God, the church as the temple of the Holy Ghost puts an end to all cultic striving to make God controllable, and at the same time to hold him at a distance by fencing him off in a sacred area, just as Jesus removed all substance from the cultic understanding of reality. Yet the church shares in the authority of Jesus only in so far as it confesses that even authority is beyond its own control, which confession, made as it is in the proclamation of his name, is not a confession of uncertainty, but of the certainty of Jesus' authority. The definition of the church as the authoritative word-event based on the authority of Jesus, must be made explicit in ecclesiology from various points of view which should not be isolated from one another.

8. Its *basis*. The church as the authoritative word-event is bound to the tradition of its basis. Although this is only accessible in the traditions of the beginnings of the church, such traditions are not in themselves constitutive for the authoritative word-event, but only in so far as they provide us with the tradition of the basis of the church. Thus particular traditions do not have the force of law; rather, in all the traditions which one has to consider, the truly authoritative (because it is authorised) element is to be found in the tradition of Jesus as the occurrence of authority, as the Gospel in person. Thus it would be a false conclusion to try to reduce the tradition of Jesus to his *ipsissima verba*, even if it were in an attempt to preserve the purity of this tradition. Now of course we should not underestimate the importance of the opportunity afforded by the synoptic tradition of establishing a hermeneutic criterion for the primitive christian tradition by determining the basic traits of the words and behaviour of Jesus. Nevertheless the point of such a hermeneutic enquiry into the historical Jesus would be completely lost if one allowed one's biographical or legal interests to become so

dominant that the stress was firmly laid on particular words and types of behaviour to the exclusion of a proper consideration of the authority which is witnessed to in the tradition, i.e. to the exclusion of that which came to expression in Jesus. Considered from this point of view, the kerygmatic tradition of primitive Christianity can be seen to be full of the Jesuanic tradition which makes explicit the authority which occurred in him. Understood in this way, the Pauline and Johannine literature can be seen to be dominated by a genuine tradition of that which came to expression in Jesus himself (e.g. in the Pauline doctrine of freedom), and this means—contrary to a superficial understanding of the historical—that it is dominated by a tradition of the 'historical' Jesus (objective genitive) seen as the basis of the church (even if in this it scarcely mentions the historical Jesus).

9. *Time*: the church as the authoritative word-event if it is to remain true to itself must be related to the Holy Spirit, by whom such authority is brought into being. It cannot hold fast to the tradition of its basis simply by holding fast to it as a religious yoke (i.e. if authority is asserted simply because it has been authority in the past) which is to turn it into legalistic authority. Yet, properly understood, it is not the tradition which has to be made present and actual, as if the Holy Spirit had to be sought elsewhere than within the tradition (as happens in the enthusiast's flight from the historical into a metaphysical understanding of the spirit). Rather it is by virtue of the basis of the church which has been handed down that the present is opened up; that is to say not by virtue of its own authority, but in its own present perception of the authority of Jesus. The basis of the church cannot as such be asserted simply in the form of scripture or of particular formulae (however important these may be for the tradition), but only by the present, free, responsible word of mouth of the man who bears witness to it. It is therefore the condition of any authoritative word-event that the basis of the church should be shown as the authorising authority, as

liberating freedom. Yet it is not for us to judge the authority of the witness by attempting to search out the secrets of his heart, which God alone can do, but by examining the Word which he speaks. The authorised Word is granted not to him who strives for authority, but to him who submits to the Word. One can neither legitimate the Word of the speaker, nor can one free oneself from the obligation of listening to it by passing judgment on the person of the speaker. When we talk of 'Word' in this context ('examination of the Word', 'submitting to the Word', 'listening to the Word') we must of course always bear in mind the situation of the Word, viz., that it occurs in time. The Holy Spirit, which is the Spirit of the Word, is not the Spirit of mere speech but is concerned with everything which has to do with the word-event. And above all with the time of its activity. The confession of the Holy Spirit belongs to the authoritative word-event; as the certain confession that the Spirit lies beyond our control it is essentially prayer and leaves the responsibility for the future of the Word, as for all the future, to God. The authoritative confession of the Word does not exercise control over the activity of the Word, but is patient and allows men time, because it is the witness to the experience of patience and the gift of time.

10. *Human relations:* the church as the authoritative word-event does its work to the honour of God among men, through men and for men's sakes. The institutional and also sectarian disregard of the *humanity* of the church, i.e. that the church is concerned, in everything it does, with men, that the church as authoritative word-event is composed of men ('to wit the holy believers and sheep who hear their shepherd's voice'[5]), is disregard of Jesus as the basis of the church, and consequently of the Holy Spirit, which means the *divinity* of the church. For the authorised word-event calls men to freedom, i.e. to the sonship of God, to the freedom to be men. It is no objection to the authority of the call-event (it rather casts light on the nature of this type of authority) that it awakens the struggle

between faith and unfaith; and it is this struggle which produces the division which for the time we observe between those who, joining their voices to the authorised word-event, confess their faith, and those who refuse to join in. This division is only temporary, in the first place because the intrusion of external factors blurs the distinction between those who confess their faith and those who reject faith, and thus obscures the language of confession; secondly, because in spite of this division every man remains till his death torn between faith and unfaith; and lastly, because the final division into elect and rejected cannot be deduced from this temporary division, and remains hidden, remains an object of faith. It is precisely from the temporary nature of this division that the struggle between faith and unfaith draws its seriousness and its joy. Whoever confesses his loyalty to the basis of the church, stands under (and this is the meaning of baptism) the sign of the authoritative word-event, not by virtue of his own invocation of the basis, but because he has been called in a way which cannot be reversed and which affects the whole of his life: and in the continuing struggle between faith and unfaith he is directed to participate in this word-event by receiving it and by sharing responsibility for it. The life of the Christian is life in the church, life in baptism;[6] it means that by being exposed to the word-event one must look for the death of the old man and the resurrection of the new. Because the church is the word-event and because therefore it concerns man as man and creates the new man, it is not concerned with an abstract individual but with man in his relationship with other men. He cannot participate in the authoritative word-event without thinking about the others who do or do not also participate. The freedom of Sonship is also the freedom for brotherhood; as such it is not enslavement to particularity but—and this alone is the meaning of the brotherhood of believers—it is the united freedom of the free for universal liberating love; it is the inbreaking of the new humanity, of the body of Christ which enfolds the living and the dead.

11. *Recognisability:* the church as the authoritative word-event must be recognisable. This because the church in its very nature is public. Nor is the publicity of the church a mere chance characteristic which can be put on or off for tactical reasons. It is identical with the authority of the Word which excludes any secret teaching and forbids the church to exist as a secret society. Naturally the proper way for the church to make itself public will depend on the particular situation, and cannot simply be guaranteed by fulfilling certain formal conditions; for it can only be achieved by the action of the authorised Word. The mere fact of holding public services in a generally accessible place will not in itself make the church public; for if they lack authority they can all too easily be distorted into a mere spectacle, into the activity of a private little clique. The catacomb meetings of the *ecclesia pressa* and spiritual advice given in private may, with regard to the authority of the Word, have the essential characteristics of the publicity of the church. Thus the question of the recognisability of the church is made more urgent by the confusion which surrounds the matter. We shall have to look not only for signs of the church's own publicity, but also for notes of the true church with regard to the confusion within the church between the true and the false church. Yet it is precisely in relation to the question of the true and false church that the notion of the publicity of the church becomes problematic. Thus any attempt to understand the church as authoritative word-event will involve us in dealing with the problem of the recognisability of the church, and while no one can deny that the church must be recognisable, it is anything but clear how this is to occur. (This is of course the traditional problem of the visible and invisible church.) Thus if we are to achieve a proper understanding of the church we will have to stress its unrecognisability in two respects: firstly with regard to the deceptive character of all the guises assumed by the church, which are not themselves authorised word-event (e.g. particular ceremonies, ordinances, activities, reli-

gious observances and so on—to use the terminology of the reformers: *traditiones humanae*); for if one were to consider these as notes of the church one would regard them as necessary and would consequently detract from the gospel. Further, considering the unrecognisability of the church as *absconditas sub contrario*: its sanctity is hidden under sin, its authority under weakness, and indeed this is only to be expected, seeing that it has its existence in Word and faith. We can therefore accept as a note of the church only that which *makes* the church the church, that is, anything of which it can be said that it is necessary to the church. This can be the authoritative word-event only on the basis of the authority of Jesus. The recognisability of this distinguishing mark shows clearly the tension which exists between a general diagnosis of symptoms of the connection of the church with the tradition of the basis of the church (the use of the scriptures, invocation of Jesus Christ, dispensing of the sacraments etc.), and the necessity of giving an accurate definition of one's understanding of the authoritative word-event.

12. *Service:* the church as the authoritative word-event issues in freedom for service. In the totality of its existence—and not merely in particular activities—it is divine service and this is, at the same time, service of man. Once we have seen this, it will of course be clear that service of man is in no sense an alternative to service of God. For this service is rendered through the authorised word-event itself, which as the presence of God is an event which impinges on men. For service can be given to God among men only through the presence of God. And in the last resort, it is only through the presence of God that service can be given to man. This then gives us a criterion for all those activities which are specifically described as divine service: God is served only by the proclamation of his presence, i.e. by acceptance of and submission to his presence; in other words, he is only served by Word and faith. This event of divine service serves to build up the church and this does not mean that it serves to build up the private life of the individual or

the private life of a community which exists only for itself, but that it must further the progress of the authoritative word-event in the world. Building up the church means the furtherance of the authoritative word-event, it means putting the church into practice as mission. The distinction between congregational worship and the organisation of missions is makeshift and superficial and must not be allowed to become constitutive for ecclesiology. Even the Lord's Supper, as the proclamation of the Lord's death (I Cor. 11. 26), is a word-event which impinges on the world. The congregation only meets together in order to free itself for its life for others, and not in order to remain together. Every member of the church therefore partakes and shares in the execution of the word-event in accordance with the *one* authoritative freedom (which is identical with faith) in the diversity of gifts—and this is what is meant by the priesthood of all believers. Thus, of the different orders within the church which are necessitated by the diversity of the gifts, we can say the following. All ecclesiastical orders are in the last resort one, in that they are all different aspects of the one authoritative word-event. Their authority is the content of the Gospel itself and makes the so-called office of the preacher (*Amt*) pure service. The criterion of all church service and of all church order is to be found in one thing alone. It is that the authoritative word-event, i.e. the liberating freedom, must be allowed room to operate, in other words that the church must be allowed to exist as the salt of the *earth*, as the light of the *world*, as sheep among wolves. The ways in which the authoritative word-event comes into effect are more manifold than is suggested by the traditional form of the church and by traditional church language. The task of ecclesiological reflection is so to concentrate on the basic relation of the church as the authoritative word-event that one becomes free and can make others free to have renewed courage, to find new ways of service for freedom. Whoever has to acknowledge that Jesus is right and cannot conceal from himself the need of men is free for this service.

VI

Appendix

1. The question of the scientific nature of theology[1]

I would like to make a few points about this, following on Schleiermacher's definition of theology as a 'positive science'.[2] If, in contradistinction to rational, speculative theology, one attempts to relate theology to a historical datum (Schleiermacher: 'to a particular type of faith', i.e. to a particular form of God-consciousness), then we must ask which is the constitutive historical datum amidst the diversity and contradictions of the christian tradition. If theology is not to be debased into a merely historical (*historisch*) science, and thus cease to be theology; if it is rather to assume responsibility for that with which it is confronted in history, then it must, as Schleiermacher himself insists, proceed by critical reflection and examination. This is indeed forced on the theologian by the historical datum itself, so long, that is, as he refuses to commit himself blindly to mere chance events or to consider the historical datum as over and done with, i.e. as not demanding that one should oneself share responsibility for it. To theology there belongs then both the element of criticism and of shared responsibility. The standpoint of positive science entails in the case of theology—and in this it is not alone!—a relationship not only to recounted history, i.e. to history which has been decided, but also to history which has yet to be decided. Thus it would be possible to go on from Schleiermacher's position and to bring together both dimensions of the concept of positive science:

the relation to the past and the relation to the future under the heading of *responsible* history. For this contains both points in bearing responsibility for past history as for future history. Instead of speaking of positive science, one could say that theology, because it is through and through related to history, is responsible science.

The usefulness of such a term would have to be demonstrated by showing that it helped to point the way forward for our understanding of the scientific nature of theology by differentiating and pin-pointing the general scientific characteristics of this study. Even if Schleiermacher considers that theology cannot be shown to belong 'necessarily to the body of the sciences, merely by an examination of the concept of science',[3] this does not mean that theology is in consequence released from the task of reflecting on its relation to other sciences and on its own character as a science, that it need not take stock of the notion of science. It might seem on the face of it that to withdraw under the slogan of 'ecclesiastical science' is to follow Schleiermacher,[4] but it would in fact be to mistake his intention. Yet if we follow his lead and substitute 'responsible' for 'positive' science, then we could bring out the differentiation within the concept of science by contrasting *calculating and responsible sciences*. This becomes clear immediately if we take the extreme case of the distinction between physics and theology. It would of course have to be carefully worked out to show the differences in scientific methodology. What binds the two halves of the distinction together is in some way indicated by the fact that in both cases, in calculation and in sharing responsibility, the understanding of one's scientific task is impinged on by the relation to the future. This indeed is true even of the pure natural sciences, in the sense that they are concerned with the discovery and mastery of calculable connections (however inadequate the traditional concept of laws of nature may be shown to be). The connection between calculating (*berechnend*) and responsible (*verantwortend*) science is indicated by the etymology of the German words. '*Rechnen*' (reckon, calculate) and

'*Zählen*' (count; *erzählen*=recount) have their roots in the same sphere of meaning as '*Rede*' (speech) and '*Sprache*' (language).[5] It is not by chance that *das zählende Rechnen*' (lit. 'counting reckoning'=mathematical calculation) and '*das erzählende Rechenschaftgeben*' (lit. 'the recounting giving-of-reckoning'=recounting and assessment of history) both point to a common root, in which the concept of *Verantworten* ('answering for', 'taking responsibility for') turns out to be the most embracing concept of all.

2. *The meaning of the word 'dogmatics'*[6]

The name 'dogmatics' seems to indicate that the subject of dogmatic theology is a particular group of texts, the dogmas—at least that is if one explains the word 'dogmatics' as the 'science of dogma or the dogmas'.[7] Of course such an interpretation still leaves a great deal open, depending on what one understands by 'dogma' or the 'dogmas', whether one sees it as a historical datum (and here again one may mean the dogmas contained in the scriptures, the *articuli fidei* of old Protestant orthodoxy, or the traditional dogmas established by the church, or the doctrines of individual theologians), or whether one sees it as a task for theology to work on.[8]

Yet even the contention that the word-formation 'dogmatics' implies, from a purely semasiological point of view, the meaning 'science of dogma or the dogmas', is at least questionable. Cf. M. Heidegger's *Interpretation analoger Wortbildungen*:[9] 'The name "aesthetics" is formed in a similar way to "logic" and "ethics". We have always to supply *epistēmē*: knowledge. Logic: *Logikē epistēmē*: knowledge of the *logos*, i.e. the doctrine of the statement and the judgment as the basic form of thought. Logic: knowledge of thought, of thought-forms and rules of thought. Ethics: *ēthikē epistēmē*: knowledge of the *ēthos*, of the inner disposition of man and of the way in which his behaviour is determined. Logic and ethics are both concerned with human behaviour and its laws. The word "aesthetics" is formed in a corresponding way: *aisthētikē epistēmē*; knowledge of the behaviour of man with regard to his senses, sensibilities and feelings, and of that by which it is determined. That which determines thinking, logic, and towards which it is directed, is truth. The disposition and behaviour of man, ethics, is determined by and directed towards the good. The feelings of men, aesthetics, are determined by and directed towards the beautiful. The true, the good and the beautiful are the object of logic, ethics and aesthetics. In this view aesthetics is the consideration of the state of a man's feelings in his relation to the beautiful, it is the consideration of the beautiful in as far as it is related to the state of men's feelings.' Now if we can interpret the word-formation 'dogmatics' in the same way, then we shall have to ask with which of man's activities it is concerned and towards what this activity is directed. And one would have to reply: with *dokein* or alternatively *dogmatizein*. And if one wished to risk fitting it into the pattern outlined above, then one would be tempted to say: dogmatics is knowledge of decided opinions, of 'faith' or alternatively of the linguistic expression of faith in assertive speech, of *assere*, of *homologein* and so of God as the one towards whom the language of faith is *ultimately* directed.

Although further reflection shows that this opinion could be supported more fully than might at first sight appear, we must counter the danger of producing an artificial construction by turning to the history of the word itself. *Dogmatik*, which is an abbreviated Germanised form of *theologica dogmatica*, goes back, as is well known, to a scientific term which was first coined in the seventeenth century.[10]

The use of the word 'dogmatic' in jurisprudence (e.g. *Strafrechtsdogmatik* = dogmatics of penal law) must have come into being at the beginning of the nineteenth century. W. Schönfeld, *Grundlegung der Rechtswissenschaft*, 1951, 122, draws attention to F. C. von Savigny's: *Vorrede zur Zeitschrift für geschichtliche Rechtswissen-*

schaft I, 1815, 1-17 ('Uber den Zweck dieser Zeitschrift') where the name *Dogmatik* is 'used so much as a matter of course as if it had long been known' that one would have to assume that Savigny had himself found this use of the word already in existence. The passage, which is also interesting from a methodological point of view, runs as follows: 'The editors would indeed feel themselves seriously misunderstood if this were taken to mean that their plan embraced only such researches as fall within the accepted division of subjects in the history of law; rather it is proper that we should be concerned here with dogmatics and interpretation in so far as they are to be treated in an historical manner, so that in fact it will be quite impossible to tell merely from the subject of a paper whether or not an article is in accordance with the aims of the journal, but only from the point of view of the writer and from the way in which he treats his subject. Equally, the editors are very far from being disposed to exclude all practical opinions from their columns, which would be to suppose that the calling of the practising lawyer and the academic lawyer were opposed in spirit to one another. Yet this is not the case: the only absolute cleft lies between the historical and the unhistorical, while the practical business of the law may be conducted with the finest scientific sense. . . . It is the triumph of historical research, if it should succeed, to present its findings simply and directly as something which one has oneself experienced; it is then that the two points of view, the historical and the practical, can be said to be most perfectly combined.'

On the other hand, as O. Ritschl[11] showed, the term *medicina dogmatica* occurred in the middle of the sixteenth century; admittedly, it was not used to indicate a separate medical discipline alongside others, but to describe a particular school of medicine as contrasted with empirical medicine. Such use goes back directly to the ancient usage: Galen speaks of *dogmatikoi iatroi* and the Sceptics (e.g. Sextus Empiricus) attacked the *dogmatikē philosophia*[12] by which in the first place they meant the Stoa, which so far as I know did not use this description of itself, but emphasized the positive sense of dogmas in the sense of prohairesis, alongside the negative sense.[13] If on the other hand, *theologia dogmatica* occurs in the seventeenth century as the description, not of a theological position but of a theological discipline, there is a two-fold explanation of this, represented by the two oldest of the known witnesses of this term: Georg Calixt and Heinrich Alting.[14] Because the subject which is now referred to as *theologia dogmatica* is not in itself new, the new terms arise from a new need for making a distinction.

Calixt distinguishes *theologia dogmatica* from *theologia moralis*,[15] whereas H. Alting distinguishes it from *theologia historica*.[16] The distinction between 'dogmatic' and 'ethical' has its roots in the Aristotelian distinction between *dianoētikai* and *ēthikai arētai*[17] and receives some support in the usage of the Greek theology of the early church as well as in sixteenth and seventeenth century Western theology. The way had also been prepared for the distinction between 'dogmatic' and 'historical' by the harmless distinction between didactic and narrative material[18] which had, however, disastrous consequences for theology with the rise of the critical historical method. The distinction between dogmatics and ethics is drawn with regard to the different subject matter of the disciplines. This would at least suggest—although it is not conclusive evidence—that the name dogmatics derives from the orientation of the subject on certain dogmatic texts which contain the *credenda*; on the Bible as the repository of the *articuli fidei* or on the witnesses of the received doctrine of the church, in such a way that 'dogmatics' itself becomes a part of historical theology. (This in some ways indicates a line of development which leads to Schleiermacher and which begins with Calixt, or even with Melanchthon.) If on the other hand we see dogmatics primarily as distinguished from historical theology—and in recent years, there has been an overwhelming tendency towards this—then the name 'dogmatics' indicates the responsible reflection on the dogmatic, assertive, linguistic event, which furthers and makes possible the cause of theology. Thus what at first sight appeared to be merely a problem of formal method, turns out to be the fundamental question of the subject of theology.

3. The use of the word 'kerygma' in recent theology[19]

There is so far as I know as yet no really adequate study of the *adoption and use of the word kerygma in recent theology*. I can only make a few points here. Bultmann's intensive use of the word in the hermeneutic task of combining the historical and dogmatic aspects of theology is terminologically and theologically a *novum*, although it is possible of course to trace its antecedents. The studies by U. Luck[20] and K. Goldammer[21] on the historical background of the use of the word kerygma in recent theological research are inadequate. Whereas older works of reference have no entries under this word, EKL II, 592-4 contains nothing about the antecedents of the term and H. Ott[22] restricts himself to the observation: 'The concept "kerygma" does in fact occur from time to time in earlier theological literature (e.g. J. S. Semler who contrasts "kerygma" and "dogma"—where of course "kerygma" is used in a quite different sense from the way in which it is used today) . . .' (1251).

I do not know which particular passages Ott has in mind. In any case I could only find one reference to this in Semler:[23] 'Right at the beginning of the christian religion people were far-sighted enough to see that it was necessary to suit their description and advocacy of it to the capacities of those whom they addressed . . . and so both teachers and catachetes were obliged to distinguish between the choice and the arrangement of truths, lest they should confuse *kērygma and dogmata*. Similarly, we cannot transpose ourselves into another age or regard the teaching methods of one age as if they were binding for all time.' Semler uses this distinction then to throw light on his central theme: the temporal relativity or rather the accommodation of the type of teaching to the needs of its age;

in other words, his theme of the distinction between theology and religion. Kerygma is then the lasting truth of the christian religion which cannot be contained in unchanging prescriptions for its teaching; it is that which must be known and believed by all, that which he frequently describes as the 'ground and content of the christian religion'[24] by which he means the 'teaching and history of Christ'.[25] In any case, I was unable to find any use of the word kerygma by Semler which was more frequent or better defined than this.

There are, too, occasional references to the word *kērygma* in the works of J. G. Herder. If Semler laid stress on the understanding of the kerygma as the basic *content* of the proclamation, Herder uses the word to bring out more strongly the oral nature of the Gospel as 'announcement', in the sense of the well-known sayings of Luther[26] and Lessing.[27] J. G. Herder: [28] 'Christianity did not start with *the writing of the Gospels* but with the proclamation of past and future things (*kērygma, apokalypsis*), with exposition, teaching, comfort, admonition, *preaching*. 387: 'All three Gospels were but *one Gospel, composed in accordance with one rule*, but subordinate to the oral discourse (*kērygma*), to the actual *proclamation of Christ,* since no one at that time entertained the idea of new Holy Scriptures.' Cf. 196*f* 381: 'So by its very nature this Gospel was *proclamation, an oral message*.' 211. 'A law is written, a joyful message is proclaimed.' 203: '. . . in the article: '*Jesus is Christ, the Son of God*', everything was contained retrospectively or prospectively . . . The way in which the different apostles expressed themselves on this subject had to be left to them; . . . yet there is *one Gospel* which lies at the root of all. The rule was in itself clear and established: for it was experienced or believed *history*.'

In both these uses, with the different emphasis on the core of the proclamation and the oral proclamation, the interest in the use of the word kerygma lies in its opposition to the old Protestant orthodoxy: on the one side it was used to attack the orthodox doctrine of the fundamental articles (which by contrast with that which was now seen to be basic had not led to a concentration on essentials), on the other it was used to counter the orthodox doctrine of verbal inspiration. It is interesting to note that the term which was first used to further anti-orthodox tendencies was later in part pressed into the service of neo-orthodoxy.

In the theological literature of the nineteenth century one comes across the word relatively infrequently but again and again used in the same way and at first still in its Greek form. It is used in various senses which are not sharply differentiated, partly to bring out the proclamatory character of the preaching as against dogmatic forms of speech,[29] partly to bring out the character of the kerygma as the sum of faith in the sense of the distinction between religion and theology,[30] partly to stress the point of view of missionary proclamation as against the congregational sermon.[31]

The more intensive use of the word dates, so far as I know, from the increasing historical interest in the oldest formulae of faith (symbolic research) on the one hand,[32] and from the questions raised by form criticism on the other hand (kerygma as the form of primitive Christianity which was used for the formation of tradition—and so at the same time the singularity and the diversity of the types of kerygma!).[33] In the form-critical notion of the concept of kerygma the different aspects, its oral nature, its fundamental christological character, its formulation, and missionary orientation are interwoven. Yet, as indeed was true of the whole previous history of the use of the term since the first traces of it in Semler and Herder (apart, that is, from occasional uses of it in practical theology), kerygma is still only spoken of historically (*historisch*) with regard to primitive Christianity.

If I am right, it is Bultmann who first successfully broached systematic theological problems, by combining his interest in form criticism with the general theological responsibility of hermeneutics.[34] It is striking then that Bultmann at first, even as a form-critic, uses the word kerygma only very infrequently, e.g. *Die Geschichte der synoptischen Tradition*, 1921, 167:[35] '. . . the kerygma, as we know it in the prophecies of the passion and resurrection in Mk. 8, 31; 9, 31; 10.33*f* and in the speeches in Acts. We have to reckon this tradition as the earliest connected tradition of the passion and death of Jesus.' Against this, the most important use of the concept of kerygma in the 2nd edition of 1931, 396*f* (=E.T., 371) is the result of his revision of the first edition. The word does not occur in the corresponding place in the 1st edition (227). When explaining the genesis of the Synoptic Gospels, he says:

1921	1931
'They needed a cultic legend for the *kyrios* of the Christian cult. In order that the schema of the Christ-myth might be illustrated, it had to be linked with the tradition about the history of Jesus.	'But their own specific characteristic, a creation of Mark, can be understood only from the *character of the Christian kerygma*, whose expansion and illustration the gospels had to serve. The primitive Christian kerygma that grew up on Hellenistic soil is represented by many passages in the Pauline letters, which depend upon the church tradition . . . as by the equivalent passages in Acts . . . The Christ who is preached is not the historical Jesus, but the Christ of faith and cult. Hence in the foreground of the preaching of Christ stands the death and resurrection of Jesus Christ as the saving acts which are known by faith and become effective for the believer in Baptism and the

	Lord's Supper. Thus the kerygma of Christ is cultic legend and the *Gospels are expanded cult legends.* [There follow some remarks on the motives for the further illustration of the kerygma.]
Which amounts to this: The tradition had to be presented as a unity from the point of view that in it he who spoke and was spoken of was he who had lived on earth as the Son of God, had suffered, died, risen and been exalted to heavenly glory. Thus *the Gospels are cult-legends.* Mark was the creator of this type; the Christ myth gives his book, the book of the secret epiphanies, not indeed a biographical unity, but a unity based upon myth.'	Which all amounts to this: The tradition had to be presented as a unity from the point of view that in it he who spoke and was spoken of was he who had lived on earth as the Son of God, had suffered, died, risen and been exalted to heavenly glory. And inevitably the centre of gravity had to be the end of the story, the passion and resurrection. Mark was the creator of this type of Gospel; the Christ myth gives his book, the book of secret epiphanies, not indeed a biographical unity, but a unity based upon the myth of the kerygma.'

If I am not mistaken, the word 'kerygma' occurs in neither *Jesus and the Word* nor in the early essays in GuV1, although as far as the actual views expressed are concerned one can see how he was preparing for his later use of the concept of kerygma. It first occurs expressly in 1929, in the first place in 'Kirche und Lehre im Neuen Testament'.[36] Also in 'Der Begriff der Offenbarung im Neuen Testament'.[37]

For an example of the consequent reception of the term kerygma in wide areas of recent theological literature, even outside German-speaking countries, we can point in New Testament studies to: C. H. Dodd, *The Apostolic Preaching and its Developments*, 1936, 1951[7]; in systematic theology to G. Wingren, *Predikan*, 1949, Germ. ed. 1955 *passim* = E.T., *The Living World*, 1960; by the same author, *Teologiens metodfråga*, 1954, Germ. ed. 1957, esp. 126-45: 'Bultmanns Deutung des Kerygmas'. Cf. further on the discussion of the concept of kerygma, G. Friederich, article in ThW III, 1938, 628-717; W. Elert, *Der christliche Glaube. Grundlinien der lutherischen Dogmatik*, 1940 (see index); H. Schlier, 'Kerygma und Sophia. Zur neutestamentlichen Grundlegung des Dogmas', EvTh 10, 1950/1, 481-507 (reprinted in: H. Schlier, *Die Zeit der Kirche*, 1958[2], 206-32); K. Stendahl, 'Kerygma und Kerygmatisch. Von zweideutigen Ausdrücken der Predigt der Urkirche—und unserer', ThLZ 77, 1952, 715-20; H. Franz, *Kerygma und Kunst*, 1959; P. Lengsfeld, *Uberlieferung. Tradition und Schrift in der evangelischen und katholischen Theologie der Gegenwart*, 1960, esp. 214*ff*: 'Der Traditionsgedanke bei Rudolf Bultmann'. See also the works cited at the beginning of the passage. In the cases where the concept of kerygma is still employed in systematic theology today, it usually is accompanied by a serious criticism of Bultmann (e.g. G. Wingren). On the other hand, many have raised strong objections against any use of the term (e.g. K. Goldammer).

4. The mere That and the doctrine of anhypostasis[38]

Bultmann's concentration on the pure That corresponds structurally, in my opinion, to the orthodox doctrine of anhypostasis, except of course that it has its place in a different field of interpretation, in historical (*geschichtlich*) rather than metaphysical thought. According to the doctrine of the anhypostasis of the human nature of Christ, the union of the two natures of Christ is only possible in so far as the divine nature alone constitutes the actual person of Christ, because it is in itself hypostatic (personal). The result of this was that in effect the human nature was not taken into account in the understanding of what constitued his person. So too for Bultmann the actual historical What and How of the appearance of Jesus is in no way important for the understanding of its revelatory character; only the That is important, for it is on this alone that the character of divine action, of the saving event, is hung. Now in traditional Christology this attempt to determine the place of the divine revelation in history is directed, in accordance with the prevailing ontology of the time, towards what in Bultmann's terminology is called the What and the How of the appearance of Jesus (this, because it is directed towards the anhypostasis of the human nature of Christ). For the result of the doctrine was in a certain way to enhance the human nature of Christ. The anhypostasis belongs to the *proprietates individuales* or unique prerogatives of the human nature of Christ as a result of the *unio naturarum*, so that the *unio naturarum* in Christ can be shown by the particular What and How of the human nature of Christ. With Bultmann, however, the attempt to determine the place of the divine revelation in history is made, in accordance with his ontology, not with regard to the human nature and its What and How, but with regard to an historical event. The elimination in orthodoxy of the actual personal quality of the human nature in favour of its revelatory character corresponds by contrast in Bultmann's case to the elimination or, more precisely, to the ignoring, of the What and How of the historical appearance of Jesus Christ, equally in favour of its revelatory character.

Common to both is the attempt to hold the human and the divine together. Orthodox dogmatics does this by setting the divine person in the place which would otherwise be occupied by an hypostasis of the human nature, in other words by a purely human person. Bultmann does it by setting God's action in the place which would otherwise be occupied, historically speaking, by the appearance of human action in its What and How. This visible What and How is not denied of Jesus Christ. What is challenged is that this particular What and How has any christological relevance; that it contributes, in other words, anything to the revelatory character of this event.

In spite of the structural parallels, Bultmann's actual theological tendency runs in some sense counter to orthodox Christology. For him the *unio* does not occur on the level of the natures, but on the level of the historical (*im Geschichtlichen*). Thus it does not appear in the specially qualified What and How of the human nature of Christ and its historical (*geschichtlich*) mode of appearance, but in the pure That, and that means in the witness to the saving event which completely eludes examination. There is only one way, in Bultmann's view, in which the revelation of God, the act of God in history, can be asserted, and this is by abandoning every attempt to accredit and legitimate the revelation by means of history, to ground the revelatory character in the historical What and How. For only through the Word can God be related to history. The act of God can only appear in history as kerygma. For Bultmann, the very possibility of speaking of the presence of God in history depends on the impossibility of forming any picture of the mere That. It is essential that one should be quite clear about the strict connection in Bultmann's use of the concept of kerygma between the concentration on the mere That, i.e. on the character of the revelation as pure happening, and the concentration on the character of the revelation as pure Word. Thus any correction which one makes as regards matters of the historical Jesus will directly affect Bultmann's understanding of Word and kerygma.

5. H. Schlier's understanding of kerygma[39]

The view that the kerygma was laid down word for word in

particular sentences has been put forward strongly by H. Schlier in 'Über das Hauptanliegen des I. Briefes an die Korinther',[40] and especially in 'Kerygma und Sophia. Zur neutestamentlichen Grundlegung des Dogmas'.[41] For the discussion of Schlier's views see: H. Diem, 'Theologie als kirchliche Wissenschaft',[42] U. Wilckens, 'Kreuz und Weisheit',[43] E. Fuchs, *Ges. Aufs.*, 1, 1959, 217*f.*, W. Fürst, 'Kirche oder Gnosis? Heinrich Schliers Absage an den Protestantismus'.[44]

In the following remarks I shall be dealing principally with Schlier's second article.

Kerygma is 'an authentic announcement and retailing of certain information to the public which has a tendency to become fixed in specific formulae'; 'the public announcement in a particular formula of Jesus Christ as Kyrios and of the events of his cross and resurrection from the dead which show him as such, by the apostles.'[45] But what is at first described as a 'tendency to become fixed in specific formulae' turns out later to be the possibility of development in the kerygmatic formula, which, as the 'principle of faith', is prior to the Gospel as proclamation (i.e. to that which is decisive in Bultmann's concept of the kerygma). This is brought out when he sets out against what is of course a caricature ('We must be careful not to see the formulae of faith as merely a later and fairly arbitrary summary of the content of the revelation for paedogogical purposes'[46]) his own thesis which distorts the matters in a different direction: 'The kerygma in this sense and the credal formula which springs from it is not a mere extract from the Gospel; it is not a secondary formula formed by compressing and deadening the spirit of the 'living' Gospel; it is not, as is commonly held, a distillation of the Gospel or Scripture, but rather it is itself the spring of the Gospel which for its part develops as proclamation the kerygma and the revelation which is expressed therein. The kerygma as the normative apostolic paradosis is chronologically, and ultimately theologically, prior to Gospel as proclamation'.[47] Thus, in these admittedly somewhat mysterious expressions, the actual revelation is seen as taking place in the transmission of credal formulae by the Risen One, and in the subsequent propositional homology of the church.[48]

By indicating this double source for the kerygma, Schlier anticipates the obvious objection that the diversity of the kerygmatic formulae did not in fact exist from the very beginning (which allows him to slip from the assertion of chronological priority to that of theological priority: 'the original and essential core of the kerygma', 493 = 217); but at the same time his chief concern is to prepare the way for his assertion of the identity of the structure of kerygma and dogma, which is introduced at the end of the essay (admittedly without any consideration of the historical problems which this raises): 'Thus there is contained in the matter of the kerygma no less than that which in later theology was referred to as the *dogmata fidei* or simply as dogma. For the two essential elements in dogma, the *veritates a Deo revelatae* et *ab ecclesia propositae*, with everything which they imply, together also form the essence of the kerygma.'[49] On this view then dogma is of the essence of the kerygma, and thus according to Schlier 'the principle of faith'.[50] That is to say, we must now formulate as follows: faith comes, not from the *akoē pistēos* but from dogma. 'The advent of dogma'[51] is the fundamental saving fact. Even if later there should be opened up a gateway to wisdom on the basis of the kerygma,[52] the immediate question: how one comes to faith: the question how one is to begin to understand this, is rejected in terms which may possibly be theologically justifiable, given a suitable explanation, but which, standing as they do without any such explanation, are open to the most serious objections: 'With regard to the kerygma, there is in the first instance no proof given, but it must be believed without proof; the proclamation of the establishment and inauguration of the new aeon must be accepted as it stands'.[53]

Now there is a good deal one could say about this on the basis of I Cor. 14. 24*f*. Above all, Schlier pays no attention to the hermeneutic question which is raised by the historical difference between the original language of the kerygma and our own. The impression he gives that the mere statement of New Testament ideas (always assuming that his exegesis is correct) has as such dogmatic character, is ominous. In fact, of course, he comes down on the side of the Roman Catholic solution of the hermeneutic problem.[54] 'This kerygma is . . . in the more general sense of the term the written or oral proclamation and tradition. In the more specific sense, however, it is the core of this proclamation and tradition which by virtue of its origin represents the apostolic witness to the self-revelation of the Risen Lord, as it was taken up, formulated and handed on by the church. This "core" is on the one hand contained in the kerygma in the wider sense of the word as a part of the kerygma as a whole; on the other it is the authentic and normative precision of the kerygma as a whole and, as such, its presentation. The kerygma in this sense is isolated in the symbols of the church which were formed alongside the oral and written tradition. Its pronouncements are by their very nature naturally (!) contained in the apostolic tradition, on which by virtue of their origin they continually draw. They occur again in fragmentary form in Scripture, and form in many ways the background on which the literary witnesses rest and by which they are formed. As regards their form, they are developed in the main stream of the apostolic tradition by the more or less express decisions of the church into an independent body of doctrine which became regulative for the tradition in cases of dispute, into, that is, the *regula fidei*.'[55] Thus we see that the thesis of the chronological priority of the kerygma as a fixed formula over the Gospel can only be maintained by insisting that the process by which this formula took shape is beyond the bounds of criticism, by insisting on dogmatic grounds that the beginning and the continuing of this process are identical.

6. *Psychologising interpretation of Jesus?*[56]

The formulations which I have offered: in Jesus faith 'came to expression'; and that on the basis of the interrelation between Jesus and faith the relation between Jesus and the primitive christian kerygma could be interpreted to show that the witness of faith became the basis of faith,[57] have earned me—and also E. Fuchs—the reproach of having reverted to the old historical psychological interpretation.[58]

Now I must admit to being unable to attach the obvious meaning to this label which Bultmann when he uses it clearly assumes. Of course our present situation with regard to the history of ideas would give a certain justification to Bultmann's polemic against 'the historical psychological interpretation', and might even explain the debasing of the word 'psychological' (with which Bultmann is certainly not in sympathy) into no more than an ill-considered term of theological abuse. Yet a proper suspicion of one-sided (particularly where hermeneutics is concerned!) slogans, and an equally proper respect for developments in psychology itself would suggest that it was desirable to inquire what is actually meant by 'psychological interpretation', a concept which is fundamental to Schleiermacher's hermeneutics.[59] It would scarcely be possible to banish psychological interpretation altogether from historical work. When Bultmann comments on E. Fuchs:[60] 'To suppose that Jesus, after hearing of the Baptist's end, must have reckoned with meeting a similar fate, is a psychological construction which is hardly convincing . . .', one has the impression that, combined with the criticism that it is an unconvincing construction, there is also the rejection of any sort of psychological interpretation as mere construction. Yet surely our concern should only be to set the proper limits on psychological interpretation, i.e. to limit it to the subject-matter of psychology. No one disputes that theological interpretation is concerned with 'the *overcoming* of psychology, or rather with finding the basis from which it can be overcome.'[61] Yet for this very reason theologians—and this is true of more than just exegetes—can scarcely afford to shun all matters of psychology from the outset and to pay them no attention at all.

We must now turn to the question to what extent we are dealing with psychological matters when we say that in Jesus faith came to expression; also when we speak of Jesus as the witness of faith and (only!) thus of the faith of Jesus. Bultmann puts forward two lines of argument:

a. On the one side he raises strong doubts about the validity of the inference from Jesus' own words and behaviour to his own faith.[62] It is not however really made clear to what extent Bultmann rests his argument on the essential 'hiddenness' of faith and on the impossibility of presenting it in an objective form (its *Nichtobjektivierbarkeit*), i.e. on the fact that man cannot infer from statements which are made 'to his face', to the 'heart' of the man who uttered them, for it is God alone who sees the hearts of men. There are echoes of this idea in the criticism of Fuchs:[63] 'he presents Jesus' bearing (*Verhalten*) as a phenomenon which can be discovered by an objectifying view of history. When he says that the kerygma has remained true to "Jesus' self-understanding", that the post-Easter faith has "repeated" Jesus' decision, he is thinking of Jesus' self-understanding and decision as a phenomenon which can be perceived by the objectifying historian.' (In the same way Bultmann criticises me[64] for making 'the same inference as Fuchs: namely from the understanding of existence which informs Jesus' actions and may be heard in his words to the personal attitude of the historical Jesus'—although I confess that I find it difficult to see any real difference between the 'understanding of existence which informs Jesus' actions' and 'his personal attitude'.) Yet when Bultmann continues:[65] 'This is clearly shown by the fact that Fuchs arrives at the decision made by Jesus by inference from the decision which is demanded in Jesus' message. The demand is simply the echo of the decision which Jesus took himself. This may indeed be correct; but what is the point of this reflection which can only spring from biographical interest?'—he does at least admit the possibility (however strictly limited[66]) of such an inference and only questions the point of making it.

b. This leads us to the other line of argument which is that such an inference—whether legitimate or no—is theologically inappropriate. It springs from a 'biographical interest'[67] and it can be objected against it that neither do the Gospels speak of Jesus' own faith, nor does the kerygma point back to Jesus' faith[68]; thus it falls under Bultmann's censure as an illegitimate attempt to legitimate faith in Jesus Christ. Yet it is important to notice here that Bultmann does not think twice about taking the statements about Jesus' faith in an objective sense and similarly about taking the phrase 'witnesses of faith' to mean 'believers who bear witness to their faith, while in fact the kerygma does not permit that one should inquire after the personal faith of the preacher.' Thus Bultmann himself sees 'personal faith' as a necessarily objectified psychological phenomenon. This might seem to contradict his own intention in combating any attempt to observe faith in an objective way, but in fact it is the condition of the possibility of such a stand. Thus for Bultmann to speak of the faith of Jesus is *eo ipso* the symptom of an untheological because psychological understanding of faith.

For this reason then we must put the question the other way round and ask whether Bultmann in his rejection of the 'psychologising interpretation' does not himself fall into an objectifying and therefore also a psychologising understanding of faith. Just as his understanding of history is conditioned by positivism because of his struggle against it,[69] the same too is true of his understanding of faith. Ultimately Bultmann seems unable to free himself from the distinction between *fides quae creditur* and *fides qua creditur* (or *quae credit*); thus he is obliged as a matter of course to exclude the latter as a psychological phenomenon from theological discussion.

Now this raises far-reaching theological problems, as can be seen for example from the following remark:[70] 'Instead of perhaps saying that the existential interpretation of the activity of Jesus with regard to his words and (as far as we can discern them) his actions, prompts man to see himself as called to faith, Fuchs reflects on Jesus' own faith . . .' This corresponds to the objection, which we have already quoted, against the inference from 'the decision which Jesus demanded in his preaching to the decision which Jesus had made himself.' Clearly one could say that what is happening here is that instead of restricting himself to the *fides quae creditur* which Jesus demanded (and that means then of course following it out in one's own *fides qua creditur*), he is reflecting on Jesus' own *fides qua creditur*. Yet Bultmann's formulations at this point raise two questions. In the first place it is noticeable that instead of saying: 'to believe', he says 'to understand oneself as called to faith'. Certainly faith includes the knowledge of the necessity of faith and consequently the understanding of oneself as called to faith. But are they both identical? Is the prompting of faith adequately characterised as the prompting 'to understand oneself as called to faith'? By no means! Further—and this is connected with the first point—according to Bultmann we are confronted by faith in the words and deeds of Jesus (and this is intended as a basic principle—we are always confronted by faith) in the manner of a call to faith; we are never simply presented with faith itself, with the reality of faith. Of course Bultmann admits that his phrase: 'the call to faith in the kerygma'[71] is open to misunderstanding. He stresses that this call is 'at the same time the offer of the gift of faith', is therefore 'fundamentally different from the demands of the law', in that 'the new possibility of existence' is offered, 'of course on the condition' that the receiver has the necessary 'openness' for it. Yet even this correction does not give an adequate answer to the central question how we are to give proper theological expression to the fact that faith is a gift, and moreover that it is the gift of 'openness', i.e. of being made open (and remaining open), of being freed (and remaining free) in one's existence; to the question how we are to give proper expression to the fact that the Word of faith has the character of permission, of pardon, of encouraging one to believe, of communicating and sharing faith. This central question on which hangs the understanding of the Gospel as Gospel, can only be adequately dealt with if one forgets the distinction between *fides quae creditur* and *fides qua creditur* and turns instead to the problem of authority[72] in which the relation of Word and faith is at its most intricate.

I confess that there is still an enormous amount of work to be done here. In this essay I have purposely only indirectly followed up my previous approach to these problems from the concept of faith, and so it is not possible now to give a full treatment of the subject of this note. It remains to set out two points of view from which a reply to Bultmann's objections could be offered.

a. Bultmann insists[73] that the 'kerygma does not permit us to enquire after the personal faith of the preacher,' and that therefore by 'witnesses of faith' we should not understand 'believers who bear witness to their faith'. If all that is meant by this is that we can neither legitimate the Word, nor excuse ourselves from listening to it on the basis of judgments about the person of the preacher (cf. above pp. 101, 9), then I would agree wholeheartedly. Yet this by no means exhausts the question of the relation of 'person' and 'subject-matter' in proclamation. For, in the first place, in matters of faith the Word demands the identification of the person with the subject matter.[74] This point would of course have to be developed and the distinction drawn more clearly. Yet it should be clear that the nature of the word-event of the proclamation of faith cannot be defined without a close examination of the way in which the preacher is drawn into the event of the proclamation, in which 'person' and 'subject-matter' are interrelated. The phrase 'witnesses of faith' becomes meaningless if one is not prepared to allow that 'they bear witness to their faith', however necessary it may be to insure against misunderstandings. I do not see how one can say anything of interest on the question of authority without discussing the correspondence of the Word of faith and faith with regard to the relation between 'person' and 'subject, matter'.

b. Bultmann[75] quotes my remark:[76] '. . . it is surely impossible, in view of the way in which Jesus speaks of faith, not to attribute faith to him as well.' The immediate context of the remark was an attack on the dogmatic thesis that for christological reasons there can be no question of attributing 'faith' to Jesus himself: *in eo fides esse non potuit*.[77] Thus the negative way in which I formulated the remark was not an inference, as Bultmann sees it, from Jesus' own words about faith to the faith of Jesus, but was rather an attack on the inference from the *unio hypostatica* of the God-man to the category mistake involved in using the word 'faith' with regard to the person of Jesus. Against this, I argued that Jesus' own words about faith (and here I was not in the first place concerned with questions of the linguistic history of the word)[78] and his own behaviour which cannot be separated from his Word, bring to expression that which coincides in his own person. I intentionally did not speak of Jesus as a believer but as the witness of faith. This was to bring out unmistakably the fact that the relation between Jesus and faith is grounded in the word-event and points to the word-event; that is to say that faith is seen not as something which can be ascertained or guessed at by inference, but as that which came to expression in Jesus. Bultmann himself in GuV I, 274 stresses that 'Jesus' person coincides with his Word.' It was precisely this that I meant in the remark which Bultmann rejects as psychologising, viz. that the point of view which sees faith as having come to expression in Jesus is the one from which we must seek to interpret not only the teaching of Jesus but also his person, for it is here that we meet 'the concentration of a man in a single point'.[79] In fact I would think that W. Hermann's notion of the 'inner life of Jesus' which when taken out of its context has been much suspected of psychologising, is not meant in this way at all and gives in some respects a very good account of the matter. For the rest, no matter from which point of view one approaches the subject, one returns again and again to the same issues. For if we are concerned with faith then we are concerned with the Word, with God, with the unity of person and subject matter, of person and work—and of course equally with the distinction between faith and Word, faith and God, person and subject matter, person and work. To be sure, this needs a fuller christological treatment; yet I am still of the same opinion as before, viz. that we shall only find the key to the problem how the proclaimer became the proclaimed one if we approach it from the point of view of faith; and this key lies in the fact that the witness of faith became the basis of faith.

7. *The question of the theological motive behind the formation of the Gospels*[80]

The question of the origin of the Synoptic Gospels and their significance with regard to 'the relation of the primitive christian message of Christ to the historical Jesus' is touched on by Bultmann in SAH 1960, 3 only at p. 13: 'The combination of historical reportage and kerygmatic Christology in the Synoptics is not intended to legitimate the kerygma of Christ by means of history (*Historie*); rather the reverse, it is intended to legitimate, as it were, the history (*Geschichte*) of Jesus as messianic history by showing it in the light of kerygmatic Christology. Critical historical study removes this light in order to gain an objective view of the 'objective historicality (*Geschichtlichkeit*) of the person and activity of Jesus'. Even the stress which the Synoptics lay on the importance of history

(*Geschichte*) for faith does not show, according to Bultmann, that the evangelists were interested in 'anything more than the mere That'. Yet what moved them 'so to legitimate, as it were, the history of Jesus as messianic history'? If they were indeed only interested in the mere That, then one would have to see the Gospels as an apologetic undertaking in the face of the doubts raised by the unmessianic appearance of Jesus,[81] i.e. it would then appear that the evangelists were not interested in the history of Jesus but in the kerygmatic illumination of the history of Jesus which was, alas, only too well known.

H. Conzelmann, to whose essay: 'Gegenwart und Zukunft in der synoptischen Tradition'[82], Bultmann refers at this point, sees[83] the theory of the messianic secret as 'the point of view under which for the first time the disparate material of the synoptic tradition was *consciously* conceived as a theological unity . . .' 'When this theory was put forward—in my opinion it is the personal achievement of the first evangelist—the traditional material was already couched in completely christological terms and in this respect stood in no need of any further theory . . . His [Mark's] achievement was not to insert unmessianic material into this framework of christological faith, but to arrange the existing christological material in accordance with the kerygma (seen in terms of the messianic secret). The idea of the messianic secret does not grow out of historical considerations about the kerygma. Rather, it is the expression of a positive understanding of the revelation . . . It is not the *un*messianic character of pieces of the tradition which troubles the evangelist; on the contrary it is the messianic character of some which gives him such trouble in setting out his theologoumenon . . . It was not a process whereby Mark collected material and then had to find a theory in order to explain the surprising elements in the tradition. Rather the idea of the secret as a *theological* concept comes at an earlier stage and allows the evangelist to order the disparate (with regard to their form!) pieces of material under a unified point of view. *The theory of the secret is the hermeneutic presupposition of the "Gospel" form.*' In this view then we have to distinguish between two different processes: the handing down of the traditional material about Jesus in the course of which this was already kerygmatically worked over in order to legitimate the history of Jesus as messianic history; and the origin of the Gospels where at least the form is seen as dictated by a particular theological interpretation of the traditional material which had already been worked over messianologically; in this the theological interpretation is formed with regard to the relation between 'the former time of the earthly existence of Jesus and the present situation of the believers.'[84]

Now of course neither of these processes does more than throw light indirectly on the interest which primitive Christianity had in the history (*Geschichte*) of Jesus. It would be absurd to suppose that the messianological working over and handing down of the tradition about Jesus was governed by apologetic motives alone. Certainly this was one factor. But the desire to 'legitimate the history of Jesus as messianic history is closely linked with another interest: 'The earthly activity of Jesus is related in order to depict the christian message.'[85] One does not legitimate the history (*Geschichte*) of Jesus messianically, simply because people still retain memories of it, but clearly because one is not merely interested in the That of the historicity of Jesus, but also in the What and the How of his appearance—of course not as critical historians, but because faith is concerned with the concretion of the kerygma. This was made more possible because the existing tradition about Jesus and the kerygmatic tendencies which governed the working over of this tradition in some way coincided so that in spite of all the tensions that existed between the two there was also a correspondence. Of course the actual place and course of the synoptic tradition in primitive Christianity is as good as hidden for us, particularly in view of the fact that on the one hand the Logia source with its roots in Jewish Christianity shows no interest in the narrative material, and on the other that the Pauline kerygma which gives us an insight into early Gentile Christianity seems equally unaffected by it.

I am not competent enough in these difficult matters to hazard any further suggestions. I would like simply to raise one question with regard to the second stage, to the formation of the Gospels themselves. There is no doubt that they first took shape on Gentile christian soil. This can neither be explained adequately by the desire to legitimate the history of Jesus as messianic history nor by Conzelmann's successful attempt to show the theological principle which governed the form of the Gospel. For this still presupposes a prior interest in the traditional material. Now how did this come about in Gentile Christianity and why did they react so differently from Paul? I think that this process must have something to do with the question of the intelligibility of the kerygma. Might it not be that the necessity of speaking graphically about the earthly life of Jesus and the satisfaction of this desire by the singular literary form of the Gospels were triggered off because, with the definitive separation of Gentile Christianity from Jewish Christianity, the presuppositions for understanding the kerygma which had been given in the Old Testament and late Jewish Apocalypticism now faded away, while at the same time the buttresses against radical Gnostic tendencies which these had provided also crumbled away? In this situation the announcement of God in the humanity of Jesus would necessarily have gained importance for the understanding of the kerygma as kerygma. Perhaps we can use here the sentence of Conzelmann which was in fact not first used in this context:[86] 'Mark gains his present understanding of the matter by turning back to Jesus . . . but in such a way that he sees that the historical distance between his present understanding and the understanding of the first christians can be bridged only from *there*.'[87]

Notes

Notes

CHAPTER I

The tension between 'scientific theology' and 'church proclamation'

1 Cf. on the other hand, H. Ott, *Denken und Sein. Der Weg Martin Heideggers und der Weg der Theologie*, 1959, 16.

2 What I have in mind here is not in the first place mere changes in world-views (which is, regrettably, the point of view which governs most discussions of the situation in which we have to make ourselves understood) but in a fundamental sense a change in our understanding of reality. What has changed is the sort of things which immediately strike us as self-evident, which impress us, which make a claim on us and bind us, which have authority, that is to say, the things we experience and the way we experience them, the things we will and the way we will them, the things for which we take responsibility and the way we take this responsibility.

3 There is here again a danger that the discussion of this point will become over-simplified. So we would stress that the distinction we have drawn above should not be thought of as a mere antithesis. The *problem* of metaphysics is not to be by-passed by adopting an historical understanding of reality; nor was metaphysics in the traditional sense affected by the problem of historicality (*Geschichtlichkeit*). For the rest, we would refer the reader to the works of F. Gogarten, especially *Verhängnis und Hoffnung der Neuzeit*, 1953, and *Die Wirklichkeit des Glaubens*, 1957.

4 I have chosen the Latin words merely as an aid to approaching the basic phenomena without any of the favourable or unfavourable associations which are normally connected with the word 'tradition'. Cf. my

essay 'Die Geschichtlichkeit der Kirche und ihrer Verkündigung als theologische Problem'. SgV 207-8, 1954, 31*ff*.

5 This term may perhaps have the disadvantage of sounding so devout to the ears of the ecclesiastically minded, that they fail to recognise in it the call to rethink our whole position which it implies. Cf. my essay 'Hauptprobleme der protestantischen Theologie in der Gegenwart'. ZThK 58, 1961, 123-36.

6 Cf. on this point the recent essay of G. Hornig, 'Die Anfänge der historisch-kritischen Theologie. Johann Salomo Semlers Schriftverständnis und seine Stellung zu Luther'. FSThR 8, 1961.

7 Of course this is not automatic. The reformation understanding of revelation is not guaranteed simply by the use of the historical-critical method. The *proper* application and so the proper *understanding* of the historical-critical method is something for which one must constantly strive.

8 We have, unfortunately, no cause these days to consider the pathos with which W. Herrmann was wont to make this point, as inappropriate. The following passage must serve as a reminder: 'When the perception grows within the Protestant church that the Bible is given us in order that in the stress of life and stilled in prayer we may listen to its words, if haply we may catch in it the voice of God speaking to our own hearts, then surely must perish the sacrilege that makes a law out of this gift of God's grace. Of course we have in view the fact that in our church such a deliberate profanation of the holy place gives itself out for "positive Christianity".' *Der Verkehr des Christen mit Gott, im Anschluss an Luther dargestellt*, 1903[4], 2 = E. T. *The Communion of the Christian with God, described on the basis of Luther's statements*, 1906, 3.

9 The phrase is borrowed from Henri Perrin, *Briefe und Documente aus dem Nachlass*, n.d., 79, where he quotes from the letter of a French officer who writes of preachers whose words 'are so empty of meaning that they are already in themselves a sort of counter-propaganda'.

10 The reference is to certain phrases of M. Kähler in *Der sogenannte historische Jesus und der geschichtliche, biblische Christus*, 1896[2], 73. According to him, 'the task of the dogmatic theologian today in representing the simple faith in Christ is to set the intellectual papacy of the historians within its proper bounds.' 110: '. . . I see it as a great advantage, not only in our dealings with non-Christians, but also in the

statement of our own basic position as Christians, that at the decisive point we should remain independent of all theology.' 147: 'Thus we insist that there should be an historical (*geschichtlich*) and doctrinal body of material on which faith is based which is independent of all scientific enquiry . . . It is, in my opinion, to this area, free from all attack, that the dogmatic theologian must lead the Christian.' Cf. 200*ff*. The rightness and wrongness of these remarks, in which there is a play of different points of view, could only be shown by a detailed examination of Kähler's thought, which is of course characterised by a strong apologetic interest. Cf. J. Fr. Schär, *Das Problem der Apologetik in der Theologie Martin Kählers*, Diss. Bern, 1940. On the actual point itself cf. W. Herrmann, *Gesammelte Aufsätze*, 1932, 314*f*.: 'Kähler seems to me to underestimate the great value which in spite of this still attaches to such historical work. At least he does not bring this point out. In the first place it has the value that, properly employed, it removes the false supports of faith. It does this by showing, as Kähler points out, that the New Testament tradition obscures as much as it reveals the life of Jesus, that it does not provide the means for a historically accurate biography of Jesus. Thus it can show the man who feels that he needs such a biography for the security of his faith, or who relies on the historical proof of certain facts (as for example the resurrection) that he has allowed his faith to come under the debilitating influence of foundations which can only stand up to the most gentle scrutiny. This is no small help; for at this point can begin a recognition that such foundations have no place in the inner life of a faith. Secondly, historical work can also lead to results which the faith which finds its nourishment in the tradition cannot overlook . . .' W. Herrmann also makes two similar points in *Der Verkehr des Christen mit Gott*, 1903[4], 63*f* of which the first is the same as the first point above, while the second reads as follows: 'Secondly, historical work is constantly constructing afresh, with every possible new modification, whatsoever results can be obtained from the records. By this means the christian believer is constantly called upon to compare afresh that portrait of Jesus which he carries with him as absolute truth, with the relative truth obtained by historical research. And this helps us not to forget that the most important fact in our life cannot be given to us once for all, but must be continually laid hold of afresh with all our soul. It helps us also to an increasing knowledge of the inexhaustible treasures of the inner life of Christ, and to a growing acquaintance with the real ways of his sovereignty over the real world. Of course we lose this advantage entirely if historical research is made to serve the ends of apologetics instead of remaining true to its own laws.' Also E. Troeltsch, *Die Bedeutung der Geschichtlichkeit Jesus für den Glauben*, 1911, 34*f*: 'It is . . . a mere figure of speech if one says that simple faith should not be allowed to become dependent on academics and professors. It is true in the case where a man feels a strong instinct which drives him to free himself from the nets of academic discourse. As a general principle it is impossible to insulate historical facts from scientific criticism. In this respect there is indeed a dependence on academics and professors, if one wishes to put it in those terms; but perhaps it would be better to say that there is a dependence on a general feeling of historical reliability which is produced by the impression left by scientific research. Nor is there any cause for complaint here. For it is not a difficulty which is restricted to an historical problem about faith. Faith in a scientifically educated world has never been independent of the influence of science.'

11 On the problem of the 'language of the church'—although it is dealt with in a different context from the present one—cf. Th. Bonhoeffer, *Die Gotteslehre des Thomas von Aquin als Sprachproblem*. BHTh 32, 1961, 116*ff*.

12 This question may give the impression of being nonsensical, but only to the persons who hold that the question, 'what is history?' has already been answered. Cf. F. Gogarten, 'Theologie und Geschichte'. ZThK 50, 1953, 339-94, esp. 342*f*.

13 See above, pp. 107*f* on the question of the scientific nature of theology.

14 Cf. on this whole range of questions my essay: 'Wort Gottes und kirchliche Lehre'. MdKI 13, 1962, no. 2.

15 I have developed this more fully in the articles on 'Theologie, begriffsgeschichtlich' and 'Theologie und Philosophie' in RGG[3] VI.

CHAPTER II

Historical and dogmatic theology

1 Cf. WuG 448*ff* = WaF 425*ff*.

2 L. von Ranke, 'Englische Geschichte. V. Buch, Einleitung'. In: L. von Ranke's *Sämmtliche Werke*, 2nd ed., vol. 15, 1877, 103.

3 Luther, *De servo arbitrio*, WA 18; 603, 11-13. 22*f*. 28*f*. 604, 25-9 = Clem 3; 97, 31-5 98, 6*f* 13-15 99, 15-20: 'For it is not the characteristic of a christian spirit not to be delighted by assertions; on the contrary he ought to be delighted by assertions, or he will not be a christian. This is what I mean by 'assertion'—to adhere with constancy, to affirm, to confess, to uphold and to persist undefeated . . . Let the Sceptics and the Academics be absent from us christians: indeed let there be present asserters twice as persistent as the Stoics themselves . . . Among christians nothing is better known or more celebrated than assertion. Take away assertions, and you have taken away Christianity—unless you regard christians as a whole as those whose dogmas are meaningless, over which they squabble stupidly and fight by means of assertions. If indeed you are speaking of associates, what could anyone assert more impiously than that he desires the freedom to assert nothing among such men?'

4 In the sense of *observantia*.

5 See above p. 105, 'The meaning of the word "dogmatics".'

6 Cf. my essay: 'The Word of God and Hermeneutics', WuG 319-48, esp. 333*ff* = WaF 305-32. esp. 318*ff*.

7 It is high time that theologians freed themselves from the polemical use of the word anthropology, as meaning that treatment of a subject which is (supposedly!) limited to the 'mere human' side of things, and which as such stands in antithesis to theology. As if one could speak of the real man by speaking of man 'abstracted' from God and 'withdrawn' from the world! Both parties suffer when theology and anthropology are set over against one another.

8 WA 40, 2; 327, 11-328, 3 (*Enarratio* Ps 51, 1532; on Ps 51.2): 'To acquire knowledge of God and of man is a divinely inspired and peculiarly theological wisdom. And the acquiring of such knowledge of God and man leads us to the conclusion that God is the one who

acts justly and that man is the sinner—so that man the criminal and the condemned and God the one who acts justly or the Saviour may properly be the subject of theology. Whatever is sought outside that hypothesis or subject, that is clearly error and vanity in theology'.

9 Fr. Kluge; *Etym. Wörterbuch der deutschen Sprache, compiled A. Götze*, 1943[12. 13], s.v.

10 'Putting them into effect' (*Ausführung*: leading out) is not intended here primarily in the sense of 'realisation', but rather, because this is prior to that realisation and determines its meaning and its limits, in the sense of leading over into the word (*Uberführung*) and so of taking responsibility for the text (*Verantworten des Textes*). Cf. WuG 347 = WaF 331. For from the point of view of theology man is seen as standing under the claim of the normative theological texts, and this means that in the last resort he is seen not as agent but as hearer, not as one called to action but to response. Cf. my essay: 'Die Evidenz des Ethischen und die Theologie'. ZThK 57, 1960, 318-56, esp. 342*ff*.

11 The similarity of this phrase to formulations of Ernst Fuchs emphasises the unifying force of the hermeneutic approach to theological questions.

CHAPTER III

Kerygma and the historical Jesus

1. The Problem of Christology

1 See above, p. 82.

2 D. Fr. Strauss, *Die christliche Glaubenslehre in ihrer geschichtlichen Entwicklung und im Kampfe mit der modernen Wissenschaft dargestellt*, 1, 1840, 71: 'The modern theologian does not have to provide the apparatus for this critical experiment himself. All the material is ready to hand in the history of the development of Christianity, in particular in the history of dogma, and the living theologian has only to collect it together. All the crucibles and retorts in which dogma was melted and distilled, all the reagents by which it was broken down, all vessels in which it fomented and foamed are there for our use and have long been in action. We need only take them as they are given to

us in the form of ecclesiastical parties and disputes, of heresies and synods, of rationalism, philosophy etc.' There follows the sentence quoted above.

3 E. Käsemann is right, *cum grano salis*, in pointing to the change of front with regard to the quest for the historical Jesus (i.e. that the liberals now deny the possibility of its success, while the orthodox appeal to the historical Jesus for support). 'Das Problem des historischen Jesus'. ZThK 51, 1954, 125-53, esp. 127, reprinted in: E. Käsemann, *Exegetische Versuche und Besinnungen*, I 1960, 187-214, esp. 189; cf. H. Diem, 'Der irdische Jesus und der Christus des Glaubens'. SgV 215, 1957, 7; H. Conzelmann, Art. on 'Jesus Christus' in RGG[3] III, 649). Yet on the other hand one should not forget that throughout the whole of the 19th century the critical quest for the historical Jesus which was undertaken by the liberal theologians was also accompanied by the (scientifically somewhat dubious) 'positive' apologetic interest of Catholic and Evangelical theologians in the life of Jesus. Cf. bibliography in RE[3] 9, 13*f*.

4 See above pp. 37*f*.

5 To avoid any arbitrary use of the concept of the mythological, it would be as well to keep to the meaning which attaches to the word 'Mythos' in its earliest use: as 'stories of the Gods' which presuppose a polytheistic outlook and a mythical understanding of time. In this sense we could banish myth by dispelling all polytheistic ideas and concentrating our attention on an event in historical time. However, if we take this concept of myth, which is used polemically in the New Testament, there is scarcely any problem at all with regard to mythology and the proclamation of the New Testament (cf. G. Stählin's treatment of this in ThW IV, 769-803). Yet this is inadmissible, for it takes the sting out of the problem which is posed by the process of introducing mythological motives into the accounts of historical events, which process modern research has dubbed with the misleading name of 'historicising' (*Historisierung*) of the myth (cf., for example, A. Weiser, 'Einleitung in das Alte Testament', 1957[4], 54. ThW IV, 799, 13). The difficulty is that this process took place in the name of biblical monotheism and of the witness to the revealing action of God in history. It is only historical thought which recognises the problem in this, its acutest form, just as it is only when the historical consciousness carries the day

over mythical thought, that it comes to a radical understanding of itself. The problems of interpretation which arise from this cannot be further discussed here. It should however be clear that with the changed outlook in modern thought we see the phenomenon of the mythological with different eyes from the ancients or the early Christians. This means that if the historian restricts himself to the concept of myth which was prevalent in those times, he will be hindered in his actual work of interpretation. The only proper and necessary way is to follow out the development of the concept of the mythological in accordance with the internal logic of the idea.

6 D. Fr. Strauss, *Der alte und der neue Glaube*, 1872[2], 76: 'The evangelists painted over the picture of his life so heavily with supernatural colours and obscured it with the patchwork lighting of so many different conflicting opinions of their own, that it is no longer possible to restore the original colours and lighting. Playing with Gods is no less dangerous than playing with fire.' Then follows the sentence quoted above.

7 The *possibility of docetic thought* (i.e. of the partial or complete denial of the human reality of the appearance of Jesus Christ coupled with the idea of his supernatural—in some sense of that word—reality which gave only the appearance of human-historical reality) is clearly anchored fully in the mythological way of thought, and, with the passing of this way of thought, has itself disappeared. It is true that D. Bonhoeffer in his Christology lectures for 1933 (written up from notes and published in *Gesammelte Schriften*, ed. E. Bethge, III, 1960, 166-242 = E.T. *Christology*, 1966) has made a brilliant attempt to show that there still remains the possibility of docetic misinterpretation of Christology: 'Docetism has clearly reappeared in recent Protestant theology, though of course in a different form. Interest now centres on the historical (*geschichtlich*) Jesus. A speculative concept of history has taken the place of the old speculative idea of God. Now history has become the support of particular religious ideas and values. History is a manifestation of supra-historical ideas. One of its values is, for example, the idea of the religious personality of man with the 'constant force of his consciousness of God' (Schleiermacher, *The Christian Faith*, para. 94). Jesus is the embodiment or support for this idea in history . . . From here on, the whole of liberal theology must be seen in the light

of docetic Christology. It understands Jesus as the embodiment of, or support for, particular ideas, values and doctrines. As a result, the manhood of Jesus Christ is in the last resort not taken seriously, although it is this very theology which speaks so often of man. It passes over his manhood and brings Jesus more than ever into the field of speculation and reconstruction. The understanding of the man as the support for a particular idea by-passes his real existence' (E.T. p. 83*f*). Yet there is a danger here of obscuring the essential difference between the docetism of the early church and the dangers of modern Christology which Bonhoeffer sets out. In the first case what happened was that extreme violence was done to the historic (*geschichtlich*) element by the introduction of the mythological fantasy of an illusory man. In the other, the reality of the historical (*historisch*) element was stressed so strongly that its relevance to faith could only be presented in a very attenuated form. It is not the humanity of Christ but the divinity which is in danger of taking on an illusory ('as if') character. There is a point of contact between the problems which these two views raise, in that in both of them the *vere Deus* and the *vere homo* compete against each other, if they do not actually exclude one another. Yet if one fails to grasp the completeness of the change which has occurred in the discussion of these problems, it is all too easy to brush on one side the questions which Christology has to face in the present age.

8 The *doctrine of the anhypostasis or enhypostasis* of the human nature of Christ has always given rise to the objection that orthodoxy, despite its own protestations to the contrary, has been guilty of diminishing the *vere homo*. D. Bonhoeffer himself argues in his lectures (which were not intended for publication): 'With the doctrine of *enhypostasia*, which was meant to prevent the separation of God and man in Christ, the dogmatics of the ancient Church already found itself fighting a rearguard action against docetism. The latter had already slipped back into the orthodox dogma of the ancient church in a refined form. In the denial of the hypostasis, docetism had retreated to a final position and held it . . . The reason for the constant deflection of ancient Christology into docetism lies in its concept of redemption, in which the nature (essence = *Wesen*) and personal character (individuality) of man are differentiated. The abstract doctrine of God and

the idea of redemption have the same presuppositions, the contrast of idea and phenomenon which we have already mentioned. The idea is substance, the phenomenon is accident; Christ the God is substance, Jesus the man is accident. The docetic doctrine of the incarnation is moulded by a philosophical presupposition. Anyone who does not free himself from this presupposition (idea—phenomenon) will seek in vain to escape docetism, whether of a cruder or a more subtle kind' (*op. cit.*, E.T. p. 81*f*). Now it is, I think, necessary to give a more carefully differentiated account of the doctrine of anhypostasis, and to take more care in coming to the conclusion that it justifies one's suspicion of docetism from the very start. Even then one can unfortunately find enough evidence for the view that there are deep-seated crypto-docetic tendencies in orthodox Christology if one looks at the way in which this Christology was developed with regard to the psychology and physiology of the human nature of Christ.

9 It has been usual, when giving an outline of the possible christological heresies, to group them under two heads: those which curtail the human nature and those which curtail the divine nature of Christ. Yet strictly speaking the *vere deus—vere homo* must be interpreted in such a way as to show that the curtailment of one leads *eo ipso* to the curtailment of the other. If we diminish the real humanity, we do not thereby stress more fully the real divinity of Christ (and vice-versa). Rather, we also undermine our statements about the real divinity, even when the diminution of the humanity occurs as the result of apparently laying too great a stress on the other side. The criterion for the proper development of christological dogma is to see whether it holds fast to the view that christological errors are not characterised by the fact that they put too much stress on one side and not enough on the other, and that the proper understanding of Christology cannot simply be achieved by finding a middle path between the two extremes. The *vere deus* safeguards the *vere homo* and vice-versa. Thus the *vere deus—vere homo* is only fully understood when it is used to bring out the true difference between God and man, and this contrasts strongly with ancient mythological analogies whose particular character is to blur over the distinction between God and man. If there is some truth in the view that modern historical thought means that we have to take the *vere homo* more seriously, then we would be able to test the success of this Christo-

logy by seeing whether it led not to a questioning of the *vere deus*, but rather to this being more clearly conceived.

10 One does well to recall that right at the beginning of orthodox dogmatics the subject of the *Filius Dei* had already been given detailed treatment in the doctrine of God. This determined decisively the procedure and understanding of the later doctrine *De Filio Dei incarnato*.

11 The phrase 'any form of world-view which allows for some sort of general belief in God' may cause theologians to turn up their noses, but they should then at least go on to ask themselves seriously how it is possible to produce a Christology without it.

12 Most of his critics fail to notice this because they do not take into account his (and their own!) position in theological history. Because they are not aware of the problems which have been pressing for an answer for two hundred years, they take fright at issues to which Bultmann is in fact only recalling their attention. On the other hand they fail to see that the real contribution which Bultmann has to make lies not in this but in his attempts to face and answer these problems.

13 Cf. Bultmann's formulation of the crucial problem—directed against the History of Religions school (KuM 1, 27=KaM 1, 15): 'Moreover, if the History of Religions school is right, *the New Testament kerygma has once more ceased to be kerygma*. Like the liberals they are silent about a decisive act of God in Christ proclaimed as the event of redemption. So we are still left with the question whether this event and the person of Jesus, both of which are described in the New Testament in mythological terms, are nothing more than mythology. Can the kerygma be interpreted apart from mythology? Can we recover the truth of the kerygma for men who do not think in mythological terms, without forfeiting its character as kerygma?' Cf. G. Backhaus's illuminating comparative study, *Kerygma und Mythos bei David Friedrich Strauss und Rudolf Bultmann*, 1956. To underline the seriousness of these questions with regard to the position of Christianity in the modern world I quote without commentary the remark of Ernst Jünger which comes from a quite different discussion: 'It is no mere chance that the idols of the powers who were defeated in the Second World War were taken from the Bronze and the Early Iron age: nordic man, ancient Roman man, the Japanese Samurai. That these powers were not victorious was in accordance with the basic rule that it is not possible to restore the

myth, that while it may well break through the crust of history like a volcano, it cannot determine the climate of the world.' E. Jünger, *'Vom Ende des geschichtlichen Zeitalters.'* In *Martin Heidegger zum 70. Geburtstag*. 1959, 332.

14 Cf. above p. 28, *n*. 7.

2. *The Kerygma*

1 See above pp. 113*ff*: The use of the word 'kerygma' in recent theology.

2 GuV 1, 206*f*: '*There is absolutely no "appreciation" of the "personality" of Jesus given*; nor can there be, for it would be a *ginōskein kata sarka*, both in the sense that such *ginōskein* would see Christ only as a Christ *kata sarka* i.e. as a phenomenon present in this world, and also in the sense that it would for this reason be a *ginōskein kata sarka*, an understanding after the flesh, which only took into account that which was present in this world. *Judgment on all things human has been passed in the cross*, in such a way that it has been passed as in an historical event. For Paul the cross is not a symbol, it is not the expression of an eternal idea. For him the naked fact of the cross means that man has to answer the question whether he will abandon himself in his security and in his *kauchasthai*, whether the cross is to become the decisive saving fact for him . . .' 265: 'Jesus lays down no teaching about his person, but says that his activity is decisive. His teaching is not new in so far as the content of its ideas is concerned; for its content is pure Judaism, pure prophecy. What is unheard of is that he should say it *now*, at the last, decisive hour. It is not the What of his teaching, but the That which is decisive.' 292: 'His [the Fourth Evangelist's] Jesus is from the start not intended to be the "historical Jesus", but is the "Word", the Word of christian proclamation. Jesus speaks and is this Word of christian proclamation, for the reason that this Word in which judgment and forgiveness, life and death are actualised as an event, is itself instituted, authorised and legitimated by the event of Jesus. Thus we need teach nothing of the content of Jesus' message except this That, which had its beginning in his historical life and continued to occur in the preaching of the church.' In his—to date—most recent deliverances on the subject: 'Das Verhältnis der urchrist-

lichen Christusbotschaft zum historischen Jesus'. SAH 1960, 3; 9*f* Bultmann does in fact discuss 'the attempts to get beyond the That', viz., 'that the kerygma presupposes not only the That but also the What and the How of the historical Jesus, and that indeed without these it can neither be understood nor believed'; however he remains firm in his conviction: 'The That alone is decisive.'

3 Indeed we can only discover the discrepancy between the historical Jesus and the primitive christian kerygma of Christ by means of an historical inquiry about Jesus of a sort which is by no means necessarily of the kind described by Bultmann as an illegitimate 'searching back behind the kerygma'. Bultmann's views on this matter are open to misinterpretation, particularly if one identifies them with the views of M. Kähler. The fact that Bultmann from time to time mentions Kähler with approval should not blind one to the very deep difference between their positions. Bultmann faces the problem of the historical Jesus while Kähler attempts to unmask the 'so-called historical Jesus' as a pseudo-problem. Yet this remark should not be taken as a denial of the very real contribution to the question made by his much quoted paper: *Der sogenannte historische Jesus und der geschichtliche, biblische Christus*, 1896[2]—in spite of its obvious weaknesses.

4 This, even though long before Herder had shown that the Gospels 'were in no sense *biographies*, but documentations of the christian confession of faith that *Jesus is the Christ*, and of the way in which he filled this role . . . They are what their name says they are': *Sämmtl. Werke*, ed. B. Sulphan; vol. 19, 273, cf. 194*ff*. Also Fr. D. E. Schleiermacher, *Hermeneutik und Kritik mit besonderer Beziehung auf das Neue Testament*, ed. Fr. Lücke 1838, 235: 'In view of the present state of philological studies it could hardly be expected that anyone would now be prepared to say that the first three Gospels could have been written by anyone who wanted to write a description of Jesus' life.'

5 R. Bultmann, 'Der Begriff der Offenbarung im Neuen Testament', SgV 135, 1929, 30 = GuV III, 22*f*: 'There is for the hearer no way back behind the sermon, whether it be to an "historical Jesus", or to a cosmic process which was played out sometime, somewhere.' 40*f* = 31: 'To go back behind the proclaimed Christ would be to misunderstand the proclamation.' GuV I, 107: 'We must make a radical break with the practice of looking for external or internal ("experiences") grounds for the

Word of proclamation.' 208: 'One may not therefore go back behind the kerygma, using it as a source to reconstruct the historical Jesus with his "messianic consciousness", his "inwardness" or his "heroism". For that would be precisely the Christ *kata sarka* who is past. It is not the historical Jesus, but Jesus Christ whom we proclaim, who is the Lord.' KuM 1, 50=KaM 1, 41: 'It would be a mistake if at this point one were to search back for the historical origins of the proclamation, as if this could provide its validity. It would mean that one wished to provide foundations for faith in God's Word by historical study.' Cf. the somewhat different statements, SAH 1960, 3; 12*ff*.

6 GuV 1, 107; '*Faith is directed to the Word and the authorised proclamation*. One can demand no other legitimation for the Word nor create any other basis for it than its own self. If it reaches us, it questions us, whether we wish to hear it or not.' 282: 'For precisely this reason God's Word has no credentials but simply demands recognition . . . For it would mean that we demanded that God should accredit himself before man.' 286: 'Any attempt at accrediting the Word is eschewed: it is its own "witness" and there is no "witness" other than the Word which could be examined and accepted by the independently minded man before he made his decision for faith.' KuM 1, 50=KaM 1, 41: 'The Word of preaching confronts us as the Word of God. It is not for us to question its credentials. It is we who are questioned, who are asked whether we will believe the Word or reject it.'

7 Bultmann reproaches W. Herrmann (GuV 1, 107) with having 'neglected *the element of obedience to the proclamation in the concept of faith* as a result of his stand against orthodoxy'. Instead of giving further references for this, we add his own qualifying self-correction, SAH 1960, 3; 25*f*, *n*. 79. He admits 'that it is misleading to speak of the demand for faith which is made in the kerygma. For this demand is radically different from the demand of the law, which throws man back on his own resources. The faith demanded by the kerygma is openness for the new possibility of existence. This openness is admittedly the condition of this new existence, for the demand of faith is at once the proffering of the gift of faith, which is really the new existence itself. It is not that one *must* believe, but that one *may* believe. Paul, for whom faith is obedience, does not command but asks. . . .'

8 Cf. H. Conzelmann's phrase which is expressly endorsed by Bult-

mann (SAH 1960, 3; 9) RGG[3] III, 651: 'If the object of faith is not itself visible in the world, then the relation of faith to the historical Jesus can never be more than a relation to a particular point: the only historical reference point is in fact the naked That of the historical "having-been-there" of Jesus.'

9 KuM I, 53=KaM I, 44.

10 Scholastic theology treats the question whether and to what extent grounds, in the sense of 'proofs of faith' endanger the purity of faith, under the somewhat surprising (for reformed theologians) heading of the rewards of faith. This is intended to bring out the peculiar nature of faith for which divine authority is constitutive and which is therefore only rewarded as faith in authority. Cf., for example, St. Thomas Aquinas. S. Th 2 II, q 2a 10: *Utrum ratio inducta ad ea quae sunt fidei diminuat meritum fidei*. It is odd to find an evangelical theologian deriding the intention of keeping faith pure by saying that it is considered '*avant-garde* these days to concentrate all one's theological pathos on the purification of faith'. H. Diem, 'Die historisch-kritische Bibelwissenschaft und die Verkündigungsaufgabe der Kirche'. *Kirche in der Zeit XVI*, 1961, 74-80. Reprinted in *Das Kirchenblatt für die reformierte Schweiz*, 117, 1961, 162-6. 178-83. The quotation is from p. 79=181. I leave it to the reader to judge to what extent H. Diem was referring to me in these and other remarks in his lecture to Zürich pastors, and also to judge to what extent such criticism was relevant.

11 GuV I, 177*ff* 282*ff* KuM I, 50=KaM I, 41*f* (following on the last quotation, p. 37 *n*. 6): 'But in answering this question, in accepting the Word of preaching as the Word of God, and the death and resurrection of Christ as the eschatological event, we are given an opportunity of understanding ourselves. Faith and unbelief are never blind, arbitrary decisions. They offer us the alternative between accepting or rejecting that which alone can illuminate our understanding of ourselves.'

12 Consider Bultmann's frequent use of the expressions 'fact' (*Faktum* and *Tatsache*), 'event' (*Ereignis*), and occasionally 'saving fact' (*Heilstatsache*).

13 I would recall here the unsatisfactory remarks in KuM I, 43*f*= KaM I, 33*f*: 'Anyone who asserts that to speak of an act of God at all is mythological language, is bound to regard the idea of an act of God in Christ as a myth. But let us ignore this question for a moment. Even

Kamlah thinks it philosophically justifiable to use "the mythological language" of an act of God.' 52=31: 'Are there still any surviving traces of mythology? There certainly are for those who regard all language about an act of God or of a decisive, eschatological event as mythological. But this is not mythology in the traditional sense, not the kind of mythology which has become antiquated with the decay of the mythological world-view.' In spite of his suggestive discussion of these problems in KuM II, 196*ff*=KaM I, 196*ff* ('The Language of the Act of God') there is still a great deal of vitally important work to be done here as Bultmann himself recognises when he says (*op. cit.*, 206=210): 'It seems to me that Christology must at long last be liberated from the tyranny of an ontology based on an objective way of thought, that it may be recouched in a new ontological terminology.' (Here I have departed from Fuller's translation—Trs.) Of course it is not a question simply of producing a new vocabulary, or a new theological grammar. We must attempt to gain a deeper insight into linguistic problems which provide the key to our understanding of reality, and in this the way is pointed forward by the understanding of revelation as the Word of God. Thus what follows in this book seems to me to be basically in accordance with Bultmann's own intentions, even if it leads to certain initial disagreements.

14 See above pp. 118*f*. The mere That and the doctrine of anhypostasis.

15 GuV I, 37: '. . . Yet if we were to inquire further about the necessity, the justice and the basis of faith, we would receive only one answer; we would be directed to the message of faith, which approaches man with the demand that it should be believed. We would receive no answer which would serve to justify faith before any tribunal. Otherwise the Word would not be *God's* Word; for we would be requiring God to justify himself; faith would not be obedience. The Word enters the world as a purely chance contingency, like any other event. There is nothing which could give a guarantee of our faith.' Even though we can agree with these remarks when they are properly understood, they nevertheless run the risk of obscuring the question of the basis of faith, before it has been clearly formulated. It is all the more remarkable that Bultmann never deals with this question *in extenso* in view of the fact that it was the primary concern of his teacher W. Herrmann. The phrase 'the basis of faith' occurs only occasionally in a positive sense,

e.g. TheolNT 1: =E.T. 1, 3: '. . . New Testament theology consists in the unfolding of those ideas by means of which christian faith makes sure of its own object, basis and consequences.'

16 Bultmann argues against the liberal appeal to Jesus (Reischle, Heitmüller, J. Weiss) in GuV 1, 13: 'It attempts to give faith a foundation which destroys its very nature, simply because it attempts to give it a foundation.'

17 See my book: *Das Wesen des christlichen Glaubens*, 1959, 1961[4], 83*f* =E.T. *The Nature of Faith* 1961 70*f*; WuG 317=WaF 303*f*.

18 In his discussion with E. Hirsch ('Jesus Christus der Herr', 1926. Cf. too, E. Hirsch, 'Bultmanns Jesus'. ZW 11, 2, 1926, 309-13. By the same author, 'Antwort an Rudolf Bultmann'. ZSTh 4, 1927, 631-61), Bultmann raises the question, GuV 1, 99: 'By virtue of what authority is the Word proclaimed among us?' His intention in this context is to show that the authority of the Word is completely independent, both of the *fides qua creditur* of the preacher, as well as of the results of historical criticism. Now it would I think be valuable from both points of view to resume the discussion of the matters raised between Bultmann and Hirsch, since Bultmann does not do justice to the problems posed by Hirsch. Even apart from this, Bultmann's view of what is meant by authority in this context stands in urgent need of further explanation. The question of contingency which was so much in the forefront (cf. the quotation in *n.* 15 p. 39) in the early days of dialectical theology (whether rightly so or not, is another question!) can at best only bring out a partial aspect of the problem of authority, without in any way exhausting the subject. Cf. the following formulations which Bultmann employs, GuV 1, 107: *'Faith is directed to the Word and to the authorised proclamation.'* 180: '. . . preaching authorised by the saving fact (*Heilsfaktum*) . . .' 292: '. . . because this Word, in which judgment and forgiveness, death and life are actualised as an event, is itself instituted, authorised and legitimated by the event of Jesus.' Now what is meant here by 'authorised'? What problems does this conceal? At least it is clear that there is a theologically legitimate 'legitimation'! When in GuV 1, 293 we read: 'The recollection of the events which happened at that time is only an appeal to the institution of the Word,' one question immediately springs to mind. What is the significance for the Word of its 'institution' and what is the significance of the appeal

to this institution for its authority? How can such a matter which is clearly so important for the Word be qualified by 'only'? Bultmann himself rightly points out that the authority and the intelligibility of the Word are necessarily connected questions. GuV I, 282*f*: 'But this is to say that the Word of God, which transcends human criteria, being essentially the authoritative Word, is for this very reason *intelligible*; that is to say that it comes home neither by virtue of its own magic, nor by demanding blind submission to dogma, or the acceptance of sheer absurdities. If it were not for its intelligibility, it could not properly be called address.' Yet the understanding cannot dispense with criteria. What positive approach to the criterion which we have to consider here is implied by the rejection of 'human criteria'? The following passage, which would need considerable development before it could stand as a doctrine of the Word, gives some indication, GuV I, 284: 'The possibility of the Word's being understood coincides with the possibility of man understanding himself. The question which is asked is whether he wishes to understand himself as directed by the Word. The only criterion for the truth of the Word is whether he *can* understand himself in this way; or better, this is the only answer which is given to the man who asks for a criterion. The task of the sermon is to present the Word in such a way that the possibility of understanding it becomes more than a theoretical question, a question of possible world-views, but that it should be perceived as a newly revealed possibility, attainable through our will.'—If 'the question why the proclaimer had to become the proclaimed One' is interpreted as 'the question of the inner necessity' (SAH 1960, 3; 23) then this means that at the same time we shall have to consider the question of the authorisation of the kerygma.

19 This would involve us in a discussion of the distinction between kerygma and theology, GuV I, 186: 'Yet since the kerygma can only be expressed in terms of human dialogue we have in principle to distinguish carefully between kerygma and theology. In practice, however, this is by no means so easy, for we can never say definitely how many sentences the kerygma includes and which ones they are.' 263: 'Christology, in the form of kerygma, of direct speech, and Christology in the form of indirect speech, of theological explanation of the new self-understanding of the believer', 'are always closely intertwined; indeed the kerygma is preached on the one hand by the communication of the

direct understanding of belief and on the other on the basis of his own reflected understanding.'

20 GuV I, 172: 'The *proclamation of Jesus* (subj. gen.) can only be termed *kerygma*.' SAH 1960, 3; 15: '. . . it is obvious that the *proclamation of Jesus* was *kerygmatic* . . . But the question here is what is *the relation of his kerygma to the church's kerygma of Christ*. Is the kerygma of Christ implicitly, if not explicitly, contained in the kerygma of Jesus?'

21 Typical of this is his thorough-going terminological distinction between the *proclamation* of Jesus and the primitive christian *kerygma*. TheolNT 1*f*.

22 Cf. ThW III, 714-16.

23 K. Stendhal, ThLZ 77, 1952, 719 (see above p. 118) sees 'that what is unsatisfactory here is the confusion between kerygma as the material concept and the kerygmatic as the formal concept.' For in his view the kerygma in the actual sense of the word is in its function unkerygmatic, while on the other hand much which cannot be attributed to the kerygma in the actual sense has a kerygmatic function (i.e. carries a message) in the New Testament and the church. Stendhal brings this out by talking of 'the unkerygmatic kerygma' and 'the kerygmatic non-kerygma'.

24 According to K. Goldammer ZNW 48, 1957, 100 (see above p. 118) the word is 'primarily used in the formal sense (*modus* and *actus praedicandi*) rather than in the material sense.'

25 Without wishing to quarrel with the rather obvious remarks which K. Goldammer makes in his admonition at the end of his essay (*op. cit.*, 101) one should point out that the general observations which he makes about the formation of concepts not only go beyond the realm of philology, but are themselves completely inadequate. 78: 'One delves in vain into the history of theology, seeking the original reason and cause for this sudden popularity (of the word kerygma). One can only conclude that it is the result of the concrete needs of theology faced by modern questions, of the pervading influence of dominating personalities, and lastly of the human inclination to mouth out impressive-sounding words.' 100: 'The modern use of this harmless expression, then, is new and we can at best find only a little support for part of this use in the canon and the older extra-canonical literature. It belongs rather to

theological discussion than to the New Testament material. This realisation brings us to the question what the purpose of the modern coining or reanimation of such superfluous and historically unfounded (i.e. which were historically originally intended in a quite different sense) artificial words might be. Why do we speak mysteriously of the "Pauline kerygma"? Why do we not quite simply and appositely speak of the apostolic or Pauline preaching? Or of the missionary speeches?' H. Diem, *Dogmatik*, 1955, 119 argues in the same way: 'The concept of kerygma in the New Testament is nowhere used in Bultmann's sense.' Cf. WuG 256*ff*=WaF 248*ff*.

26 The following essays are of fundamental importance for this discussion: 'Der Begriff der Offenbarung im NT', 1929, SgV 135=GuV III, 1-34=EaF 58-91. 'Kirche und Lehre im NT', 1929, GuV I, 153-87. 'Die Bedeutung des geschichtlichen Jesus für die Theologie des Paulus', 1929, GuV I, 188-213. 'Der Begriff des Wortes Gottes im NT', 1931, GuV I, 268-93. But of course we will be dealing with points of view which occur again and again in the work of Bultmann. In each case I have merely selected a few characteristic formulations and passages. GuV I, 186: 'challenge which demands obedience'. 273: 'challenge, call to decision'. Also SgV 135, 12.30=GuV III, 7.22=EaF 64.78. GuV I, 172. 175.269.282.

27 GuV I, 272: 'God's Word does not speak to the intellect, but to the will.'

28 GuV I, 298: '. . . this corresponds to the fact that the christian kerygma speaks to the conscience (2 Cor. 4. 2). This is what enables the kerygma to be a call to decision and faith to be the decision itself.' Also SgV 135, 30=GuV III, 22 GuV I, 282.

29 SgV 135, 39*f*=GuV III, 30=EaF 86: 'Revelation does not mediate a world-view, but rather addresses the individual as an existing self. That he thereby learns to understand himself means that he learns to understand his now, this moment, as a now that is qualified by the proclamation.' GuV, I, 109: 'It (the proclamation) qualifies . . . our life in a new way, in one way or another, for "life" or for "death".' 161: 'What is "new" in this, is not *what* is said, some new message which can be grasped as an eternal "truth", but the very fact *that* it is said. It is this which makes my situation new, and myself—depending on which way I decide—a new person.' Also GuV I, 204. 283.

30 SgV 135, 29=GuV III, 21=EaF 78: 'Thus revelation must be an occurrence that directly concerns *us*, that takes place in ourselves; and the Word, the fact of its being proclaimed, must itself belong to the occurrence.' 30=22=78: '. . . it is understood in its true character only when it is understood as something that takes place in the present, in my particular present.'

31 GuV I, 286: '. . . the content of the Word as address is forgiveness, justification, life. Yet is not the Word of the New Testament more than just a challenge? Does it not also communicate something not only about the grace of God which is now offered to man, but also about *an historical* (*geschichtlich*) *fact*: the event of Jesus Christ? Thus we must consider the question: how are challenge and communication related, or how is the event of Jesus Christ which lies in the past related to the event of the challenge which occurs in the present?' 173*f*: '. . . man is understood in his historicity (*Geschichtlichkeit*) . . . so that the facts to which his attention is drawn also demand of him that he should resolve himself one way or another, force him to make a decision.' SgV 135, 25=GuV III, 18=EaF 75: 'Thus revelation consists in nothing other than the fact of Jesus Christ.' GuV I, 107: W. Herrmann 'overlooks the fact that the proclamation speaks of Jesus as an historic fact (even if it cannot be proved historically as a fact which decisively qualifies our own historic (*geschichtlich*) existence.' 176: '. . . clear that the kerygma of Paul proclaims a fact: Jesus Christ . . .' 259: 'The new life is *an historical* (*geschichtlich*) *possibility because of the saving event, and becomes a reality when it is grasped by man's decision*.' 332: Jesus Christ 'is the eschatological act of God.' GuV II, 257=EPaT, 286: 'Jesus Christ is the eschatological event as the man Jesus of Nazareth and as the Word which resounds in the mouth of those who preach him.' Also GuV I, 146. 177, 208. 261. TheolNT 43*f*=E.T. I. 42*f*.

32 SAH 1960, 3; 8: '. . . the kerygma contains the paradoxical assertion that an historical event—viz. the historical Jesus and his history—is the eschatological event (the beginning of the new aeon and all that that involves). GuV II, 257=EPaT 286: 'All that is true only if it is understood—from the standpoint of the natural man—as a paradox.' SgV 135, 28=GuV III, 20=EaF 76*f*: '. . . this revelation that takes place in preaching is paradoxical in so far as what is evident to the eye of the natural man is not life, but only death.' GuV I, 91*f*: 'The only

paradox of which we can properly speak in theology, does not consist in inconceivable and absurd thought, in irrational statements, but in an *event*, the action of God who forgives sins in Christ. There is nothing here which is paradoxical and offensive to the understanding. For anyone, if he has a mind to it, can understand what is meant by forgiveness; but that God actually has forgiven us is something which we can never comprehend, we can only believe it.' Cf., for Bultmann's concept of the paradox: H. Schröer, 'Die Denkform der Paradoxalität als theologisches Problem. Eine Untersuchung zu Kierkegaard und der neueren Theologie als Beitrag zur theologischen Logik'. FSThR 5, 1960.

33 GuV 1, 175, cf. 286*ff*.

34 While on the one hand we speak of the kerygma as address, we shall always have to stress that it is an address which is rooted in 'the factual'. This is also the case in the proclamation of Jesus. GuV 1, 172*f*: 'In so far as it proclaims a future fact, the coming of the Reign of God, yet a fact which is not seen as being of this world . . .' This must of course be taken in conjunction with the distinction which Bultmann makes between Jesus' proclamation and the prophetic proclamation, GuV 1, 174 (cf. also 204): 'Jesus gave no express teaching *about his own person*. On the other hand he stressed the importance and the decisiveness of the fact of his person, because he is the bearer of the Word in the last, decisive hour . . .' On the distinction between the proclamation of Jesus and Paul see GuV 1, 201*f*. On the relation of the Word of God and history in OT and NT see GuV 1, 286*ff*.

35 Cf. TheolNT 1*f*=E.T. 1. 3*f*. On the question of implicit Christology see above pp. 69*ff*.

36 According to GuV 1, 279*f* the concept 'Word of God' is used in an overwhelming majority of cases in the New Testament to refer to the christian kerygma. 335: 'If it is Jesus Christ alone who, as God's eschatological act of forgiveness, is God's Word to men, then one can say that all words which help to make this Word intelligible by bringing man into a situation in which he can understand it and by developing his understanding of life in that situation, are *in an indirect way God's Word*.'

37 GuV 1, 208*f*: N.B. especially: 'The kerygma proclaims . . . an historical (*geschichtlich*) fact . . . it belongs itself to the fact . . . because the That, the Here and the Now, the factualness of the person, consti-

tute the revelation. Yet for this very reason the kerygma is neither the vehicle of timeless ideas, nor the mediator of historical knowledge, but the decisive thing is his That, his Here and Now, in which that Here and Now are actualised in the address.'

38 The formulations which Bultmann himself uses when giving a description of the content of the kerygma usually lean very heavily on biblical phrases or else are theological abbreviations which attempt in an uninterpreted way to give the character of the primitive christian way of thought. Cf. for example: Jesus Christ, the Crucified and Risen One, God's eschatological saving act.

39 The beginnings of this tension can already be seen in the realm of the New Testament literature and are of course considered by Bultmann wherever they occur. He does not however, as far as I can see, take them into account in his general consideration of the nature of the kerygma.

40 GuV I, 186: '. . . christian theology . . .in its critical polemical form . . . is . . . indirect speech; in it the kerygma is present in the form of the doctrine which is being debated. So it is clear that *this theology must also in turn be subject to criticism*, although only to criticism which in its turn is grounded in obedience . . . Yet the kerygma is subject to no criticism; it is an address which demands obedience, and which cannot be judged from a neutral stand-point, for it demands the surrender of one's own judgment.'

41 Bultmann himself points this out in a similar context, see above p. 40, *n.* 19 TheolNT 580*f*=E.T. TheolNT II, 239*f*: 'For both the kerygma and faith's self-understanding always appear in the texts, so far as they are expressed in words and sentences, already interpreted in some particular way—i.e. in theological thoughts. . . Therefore, it is not possible simply and sharply to distinguish kerygmatic statements in the New Testament from theological ones, nor to derive from the New Testament a self-understanding not formulated in theological statements. Nevertheless, he who sets forth a New Testament theology must have this distinction constantly in mind and must interpret the theological thoughts as the unfolding of the self-understanding awakened by the kerygma, if he is to avoid conceiving them as an objectifying kind of thought cut loose from the "act of living . . .".'

42 See above p. 37, *n.* 5.

43 ThW vi, 209*ff*.

44 cf. WuG 326*ff*=WaF 311*ff*.

45 See above pp. 120*ff*, H. Schlier's understanding of kerygma.

46 Here we would agree with U. Wilckens' remark (KuD 3, 1957, 104): 'Most of the different formulae of the primitive christian kerygmatic tradition which have been preserved are in character more homological than kerygmatic.'

47 E.g. C. H. Dodd, *The Apostolic Preaching and its Developments*, 1951[7], 7: 'Teaching (*didaskein*) is in a large majority of cases ethical instruction. Occasionally it seems to include what we should call apologetic, that is, the reasoned commendation of Christianity to persons interested but not yet convinced. Sometimes, especially in the Johannine writings, it includes the exposition of theological doctrine. Preaching, on the other hand, is the public proclamation of Christianity to the non-christian world. The verb *kēryssein* properly means "to proclaim" . . . Much of our preaching in church at the present day would not have been recognised by the early Christians as *kērygma*. It is teaching, or exhortation (*paraklēsis*), or it is what they called *homilia*, that is, the more or less informal discussion of various aspects of christian life and thought, addressed to a congregation already established in the faith.' We can see how easily this distinction can be confused if we look at the similar distinction drawn by Basil the Great between *kērygma* and *dogma*. The former is used to denote teaching with a principally practical application which is given to the uninitiated and which can be handed down in literary form, while the latter denotes esoteric doctrine which must be preserved from the contempt of the uninitiated and can only be handed on in unwritten form: *De spiritu sancto* c. 27, MPG 32, 189 B: *'Allo gar dogma kai allo kērygma. To men gar siōpatai, ta de kērygmata dēmosieuetai.'* cf. H. Dörries, *De Spiritu Sancto. Der Beitrag des Basilius zum Abschluss des trinitarischen Dogmas*, AAG 3rd Series no. 39, 1956, 72*f* 121-28. 181-4.

48 ThW vi, 209.

49 P. Lengsfeld (see below p. 118), giving an account of Schlier's position, writes, 59: '. . . it is only the central formula which is developed in the proclamation, which arouses faith and forms the congregation. The formulation is deceptive. It is intended to give the impression that the kerygma as the central formula of the faith arouses faith.' Yet he

also admits that it is not the central formula as such which arouses faith, but the formula which is developed in the proclamation. This clearly indicates the kerygma in the sense of an address made here and now.

50 The only exception is I John 5.10: *eis tēn marturian*, but even this corresponds to *eis ton uion tou theou* in v. 10*a*.

51 H. Braun, 'Der Sinn der neutestamentlichen Christologie'. ZThK 54, 1957, 341-77, esp. 368. 371. Reprinted in H. Braun, *Gesammelte Studien zum Neuen Testament und seiner Umwelt*, 1962, 243-82, esp. 272. 273. 275. 276.

52 See above p. 38, *n.* 11. KuM II, 188: 'Demythologising, with its criticism of the world-view of the Bible, removes the offence which this necessarily causes modern man. Yet in doing so it clears the way for the real offence by which man, modern or otherwise, is confronted in the Bible.' 190: 'This is on all fours with the way in which—think of the sermons which one occasionally hears preached on Trinity Sunday!—people talk of the mystery of the Trinity which passes human thought and understanding, when the concept of mystery is taken to have its place in an objective way of thought. Here the Trinity has become a mere *x* for which neither the preacher nor the congregation can supply any meaning; they reproduce, or accept, an unintelligible dogmatic formula from the tradition. God's mystery is not an *x*, whether we think we can solve the equation or whether we think it must remain unknown.' 'Demythologising, coupled with a programme of existential interpretation, is intended to lay bare the real mystery of God in its true incomprehensibility. Understanding is something different from giving a rational explanation.' See also E. Fuchs, 'Das entmythologisierte Glaubensärgernis'. In: *Ges. Aufs.* I, 1959, 211-36, esp. 230*ff*. Particularly valuable is his distinction, 231: '*The offence lies in faith itself*. For faith is an understanding assent, says Bultmann. That is already half the offence. For unbelief is only understanding refusal in the sense that it opts for another understanding of itself. Unfaith is not really understanding refusal, but incomprehension, darkness; but an incomprehension which deems itself wisdom; a darkness which claims to be light. This is why faith becomes an object of offence for unbelief, even if only in a half-hearted way; for unbelief thinks itself superior to faith. . . Of course, for faith itself, faith is not an offence, but rather comfort and joy. It is the believer who becomes the offence to faith. The

offence here is simply that the believer can see that he is not as he ought to be. This is the motive for the fifth petition of the Lord's Prayer. In this sense the believer is in full 'control' of himself. This is the *complete* offence. . . .'

53 GuV II, 257=EPaT 285. The significance of the titles of Jesus lies in the fact 'that they give expression to the way in which the world and man have been called into a new situation by the appearance of Jesus, and so have been called to a decision for or against God, that is, therefore, for or against the world; and how the believers who have achieved the decision against the world and for God, are taken out of the world, withdrawn from the world . . . Finally, the titles all designate Christ as the eschatological event.'

54 I have the same sort of thing in mind here, which I have elsewhere expressed by the distinction between the exposition (*Auslegung*=lit. laying out) and the execution (*Ausführung*=lit. leading out): WuG 347=WaF 331. See above p. 31.

3. The historical Jesus

1 Cf. the title of J. M. Robinson's book in the next note. The questions which are being asked about the historical Jesus are certainly 'new' by comparison with Bultmann's position (and with subtle differences, by comparison with the whole movement of the dialectical theology which turned its back on liberal theology and the Ritschlean school). Yet it is only 'new' in a relative sense, since, on the one hand, Bultmann himself was concerned with the question of the historical Jesus, and on the other, because those of his pupils who have embarked on the 'new quest' owe him a great debt precisely at this point. We shall have to be very careful when we try to see in what way the questions now raised about the historical Jesus are new by comparison with the old quests of the former 'liberal' school (if we can lump them together in this way). It is not enough to say that whereas before the accent was laid on the antithesis between the historical Jesus and the kerygmatic Christ; now it lies on the unity of the two (see above p. 61 *n*. 30). Nor is it of much value to resort to sweeping and confusing slogans like 'neo-liberalism' which stress the similarity or even the identity of the questions raised. Cf. the essay which appeared in the ZThK 59, 1962 by

Van A. Harvey and Schubert M. Ogden, 'Wie neu ist die "neue Frage nach dem historischen Jesus"?' It seems to me that when we look back at the old quest for the historical Jesus we should treat it with greater fairness by asking at least what the theological motives were which inspired it. Even the so-called 'liberal' quest for the historical Jesus should really be seen as an important symptom of the efforts which were made to face hermeneutic questions with regard to Christology and to the christian preaching.

2 Without giving a detailed bibliography, I would refer to: J. M. Robinson, *Kerygma und historischer Jesus*, 1960 (a translation and revision of: *A New Quest of the Historical Jesus*, 1959). R. Bultmann, 'Das Verhältnis der urchristlichen Christusbotschaft zum historischen Jesus'. SAH 1960, 3; E. Fuchs, *Ges. Aufs.* II. 'Zur Frage nach dem historischen Jesus'. 1960. Also the incredibly mixed and confusing collection of essays in: *Der historische Jesus und der kerygmatische Christus. Beiträge zum Christusverständnis in Forschung und Verkündigung*, ed. H. Ristow and K. Matthiae. 1961.[2] Since this book is intended as a work of systematic theology it is not possible within its limits to give a full treatment of the whole range of the problem and discussion. I shall therefore follow the pattern which I have already established, and concentrate in the first place on a discussion of Bultmann's position and in particular of his most recent contribution to it, here quoted above.

3 Cf. E. Fuchs' remark in the foreword to *Ges. Aufs.* II: 'Once we used to interpret the historical Jesus with the help of the primitive christian kerygma, now today we interpret this kerygma with the help of the historical Jesus—both ways of interpretation are complementary.'

4 Cf. WuG 300*ff*=WaF 288*ff*.

5 SAH, 1960, 3; 6: 'However, I do not intend to discuss here the question how far this change has sprung naturally from the course of the debate and how far it has been guided by dogmatic interest.' It is an open question whether there is an implied criticism in this remark. There would indeed be cause for criticism if dogmatic interests were allowed to distort historical results or to put certain questions beyond criticism. Nevertheless a grasp of the theological issues which are involved can help to determine the appropriateness of the question, particularly in this case, and can therefore be of benefit to historical and exegetical studies. For the rest, it is not possible to separate the course

of (historical) research from the factors which determine the course of dogmatic discussion, which means, too, that the course of historical research cannot be separated from the course of dogmatic discussion.

6 *Ibid.*, 26: '. . . if by means of an existential interpretation we rediscover the meaning of such sayings (II Cor. 5. 17 etc.) in the sayings and actions of the historical Jesus, as in fact Braun and Robinson do, then it should be clear that we are led to this interpretation by the kerygma in which the paradox of "life in death" was first made explicit.' This is indisputably true, but it is also true *mutatis mutandis* in a more general hermeneutic context. The important thing is that this 'rediscovery' is a rediscovery of *something*, and that the difference which nevertheless exists between the two should not be obscured.

7 E.g. GuV 1, 3: 'Historical science could not possibly lead to a result which could provide a foundation for faith, for all *its results are only relatively true*.' This is certainly true of the absurd attempt to 'prop up' faith by proving historical facts. We should not, however, because of this give the impression of denying the theological importance of critical historical work which aims at a correct understanding of the text, which, since it is concerned with the Word, at least indirectly affects faith. To say that the determination of the origins of the Bible by historical methods is of no concern to the preacher in the pulpit (GuV 1, 100), may in its context be directed against a misconception of the grounds of authority and against a false understanding of the particular situation of the preacher. Nevertheless the actual form of words used is highly dangerous. Or cf. KuM 1, 147: 'It lies in the very nature of the tradition of the kerygma that one may not inquire after the historical reliability of that which is handed down. Otherwise the very eschatological event itself of which the kerygma speaks would be drawn into the relativity of all historical knowledge.' Again the first point is inspired by a polemical interest. Without it, however, the sentence is simply false. Yet with regard to the consequence of such an inquiry, one might well ask whether such consequences can be avoided by simply forbidding the inquiry.—cf. also above p. 45, *n*. 40, 41.

8 This is in no way contradicted by pointing out that the eschatological resurrection is predicated of an historical person, with regard to the fact of his death, not in the sense of an historic future, but as an act of God in the perfect present. The fact that the conceptions and

means of expression of primitive Christianity were not determined by historical thought but were historically naïve, or rather unhistorically naïve, is obvious. This is however no reason for feeling ourselves superior. It is our fate to live in an age which thinks differently, but this in itself neither brings us closer to nor farther away from the substance of Gospel.

9 SAH 1960, 3; 11*f*: 'The point which is likely to cause the most embarrassment for those who make this attempt to reconstruct the portrait of the character of Jesus is the fact that we cannot know *how Jesus regarded his end, his death* . . . The possibility that he completely broke down cannot be glossed over.'

10 See above p. 37, *n*. 5.

11 See above pp. 44*f*.

12 Cf. the title of Bultmann's paper: 'Das Verhältnis der urchristlichen Christusbotschaft zum historischen Jesus'.

13 See above p. 39, *n*. 18.

14 This is particularly noticeable in SAH 1960, 3. e.g., 13: 'The task of historical critical research is described as being 'to show objectively the "objective historicity" of the person and work of Jesus.' 13*f*: The critical historical analysis of the Synoptics is concerned with 'the question of the objectively ascertainable history of Jesus'.

15 Cf. the unhappily vague passing remarks in SAH 1960, 3; 18: 'The way forward seems to lie with those who seek to replace the objectifying historical critical study of the work of Jesus by an *interpretation of history based on an historic, i.e. existential* (*geschichtlich*, *existentiell*) *encounter with history*. Or rather they seek not so much to replace it, but to complete its work, to take the investigation a stage further. For the interpretation seeks to grasp the self-understanding which lies behind, or prevails within the historic phenomena which can be perceived by objectifying sight . . . History is understood as address, and it consists in *hearing* and not in *looking* on from a distance.' I am completely in sympathy with the intention expressed in this passage. Yet it seems to me wrong to make a clear-cut distinction between on the one hand the historical critical method, looking on from a distance, and on the other existential interpretation, hearing the address. For this seems to me to do justice neither to the internal unity of the hermeneutic process, nor to the differentiations within this process. However, before we could

discuss this point more fully we would have to take a much closer look at Bultmann's concept of history. H. Ott (*Geschichte und Heilsgeschichte in der Theologie Bultmanns*, BHTh 19, 1955; and 'Die Frage nach dem historischen Jesus und die Ontologie der Geschichte'. ThSt 62, 1960) has given the fullest treatment of this. Although my views coincide with Ott's at many points, there is a great deal more with which I cannot agree.

16 WuG 307*f* = WaF 294*f*. Also: see above pp. 124*ff*. Psychologising interpretation of Jesus?

17 cf. E. Fuchs, *Ges. Aufs.* I, 281*ff*.; III, 379. 424ff.

18 Bultmann can on occasion say, GuV I, 274: '. . . that the person of Jesus is contained without remainder in his Word, and this means too, that his Word is an event. . . .'

19 SAH 1960, 3; 6.

20 *Ibid*., 6.

21 *Ibid*., 6*f*.

22 *Ibid*., 8*f* should be compared with 15*f*. For this see above pp. 60*f*.

23 Aristotle defines continuity (*to syneches*) as unity on the basis of adjacency. Met. K. XI, 12 1069 a. This can be translated as follows (Eng. translation based on P. Gohlke: Aristotle, *Die Lehrschriften* V, 1951, 353): 'There is a continuous connection between things which border on or touch each other. One speaks of this continuous connection when the boundaries of the two things along which they touch one another and connect with each other, coincide; this means that there is continuity in cases, in which something has become by nature a unity with that which it touches.'

24 I have used it myself in *Das Wesen des christlichen Glaubens*. 1961[4] 66*ff* = *The Nature of Faith*, p. 58*ff* and in WuG 312*f*. = WaF 299*ff*, but with reservations.

25 Historic relationships must not be seen simply in terms of a physical causal nexus. The literal sense of continuity points to a great variety of possible ways in which two things can be adjacent or follow from one another in such a way that unity of connection occurs. H. Aubin's essay, 'Zur Frage der historischen Kontinuität im Allgemeinen'. HZ 168, 1943, 229-62, is concerned principally with the problem of the continuing influence of classical culture in the Middle Ages and contributes nothing to the general clarification of the concept.

26 SAH 1960, 3; 7*f*. Bultmann counters the mistaken view that he has destroyed the continuity between the historical Jesus and the kerygma: '. . . it does not in the least follow from my stressing the discrepancy between the historical Jesus and the Christ of the kerygma, that I have thereby destroyed the continuity between the historical Jesus and the early christian proclamation . . . It is self-evident . . . that the kerygma presupposes the historical Jesus, however much it may have mythologised his figure. Without the historical Jesus there would be no kerygma. To this extent the continuity is self-evident.'

27 The train of Bultmann's argument shows very clearly how one problem proceeds from another. *Ibid.*, 9: 'Does what we have already said about the continuity take us any further than the indubitable fact that the kerygma presupposes the historicity of Jesus? That is, does it go beyond the That of his history? Does this tell us anything about the continuity of the kerygma with the What and How of his history?

This is the great problem: what is the relation between the content of the work of Jesus and the content of the kerygma? *Is the historical Jesus identical with the Christ of the kerygma?*'

28 *Ibid.*, 6.

29 *Ibid.*, 5.

30 *Ibid.*, 6.

31 *Ibid.*, 10: He suggests that its exponents are still attempting 'to save something from the ashes' after the failure of the quest for the historical Jesus. 12: 'Yet however much we may grasp the "figure" of Jesus by historical critical study . . . what has really been gained? Does it really give us a legitimation for the kerygma which proclaims the historical Jesus as the Christ who died for us?' 13: See above p. 63, *n*. 36. 14: Historical criticism is not capable of 'affording a proof that the historical continuity between Jesus and the kerygma is in the nature of a material agreement. The enterprise ends in the unnecessary attempt to prove the legitimacy of the kerygma.' Of course we would not want to deny that in many cases the quest for the historical Jesus is made to serve apologetic interests which are by and large out of place here.

32 *Ibid.*, 11.

33 *Ibid.*, 23*f*: 'If a proper historical interpretation makes the Now of that time into the Now of today, and if therefore the historian can lead his hearer (or reader) into a situation where he must make a deci-

sion about Jesus on the basis of his existential encounter with the history of Jesus, does this not mean that the kerygma of Christ has lost its point, that it has become superfluous?' On the contrary, I would say that it is only then that the kerygma of Christ becomes meaningful.

34 *Ibid.*, 25: 'The solution to the problem is that the kerygma has transformed the "once" of the historical Jesus into the "once-for-all"; in other words the earliest community understood *the history of Jesus* with increasing clarity *as the decisive eschatological event* which as such can never become merely past, but remains *present* and present moreover *in the proclamation*.

35 Cf. *ibid.*, 10*f*.

36 Bultmann would of course entirely agree with this point of view. Yet the polemic which he wages does not permit him to stress this point himself. Cf. *ibid.*, 13: 'The attempt to prove the legitimacy of the kerygma by scientific investigation is guided by a modern interest in history. It puts a question to the kerygma which is quite foreign to it. The kerygma is not interested in objective history beyond the simple That. It asks for faith in Christ the Crucified and the Risen, and it is from this standpoint that it understands the history of Jesus, so far as it is interested in it at all. Paul and John are not, though the Synoptics are.' There is no time to mention here the considerations which could justifiably be set out against the misuse of the historical method.

37 W. Anz seems to restrict the quest of the historical Jesus to this misleading conception, when he sees it as being inspired by a 'concern for the continuity of the event of proclamation.' 'Verkündigung und theologischer Reflexion'. ZThK Supp. 2, 1961, 71.

38 Behind this pseudo-orthodox tendency lies the absurd notion that christological kerygma would be more intelligible and more convincing in the mouth of Jesus than of the Apostles.

39 Yet this view is also, in its own way, pseudo-orthodox. To be sure it decks itself out in orthodox colours by deriving everything from the 'fact of the resurrection', and yet it misses the main point of christological orthodoxy: that Jesus did not become the Son of God only after his death, but that he, the historical Jesus, was and is the Son of God. Cf. WuG 314*f* = WaF 301*f*.

40 Yet of course even such a minimal abstract historical definition already implies a great deal about the content of the definition. For we

are not concerned with a physical but with an historical definition in time and space.

41 Cf. WuG 301.

42 See above pp. 49*ff*.

43 See above p. 52.

44 See above p. 48, *n*. 51.

45 SAH 1960, 3; 6*f*.

46 *Ibid*., 6.

47 *Ibid*., 26. Also 17: 'The Christ of the kerygma has, as it were, crowded out the historical Jesus . . .' Whereas Bultmann normally speaks of 'the Christ present in the kerygma' (*ibid*., 27), we occasionally find the expression 'that Jesus is really present in the kerygma' (*ibid*., 27). There is a particularly striking phrase in GuV II, 260=EaF 289: '. . . the eschatological event as the event of the christian message, in which the historical Jesus becomes present.' The contrary view seems to be expressed in GuV I, 208: 'It is not the historical Jesus but Jesus Christ, the preacher, who is the Lord.'

48 E.g. GuV I, 200: 'Paul waits for the fulfilment but in a different way from Jesus. Jesus looks to the future, to the *coming* rule of God—although admittedly to the rule of God which is coming and breaking in *now*. Paul looks back: *the beginning of the new age has already come to pass*.' 201: '. . . the difference lies . . . not in the diversity of ideas or concepts, but in the fact that Paul sees things which for Jesus were in the future, as in the present, or rather in a present time which was inaugurated in the past; this is not because he judges the times from a different general or "religious" standpoint from Jesus, but because he is of the opinion that a decisive event has created a new time.' Cf. 'Jesus und Paulus'. In: 'Jesus Christus im Zeugnis der Heiligen Schrift und der Kirche'. Supp. 2 EvTh 1936, 84. The same is to be found—admittedly only as a 'rough sketch'—in SAH 1960, 3; 6: 'Jesus proclaims the eschatological message of the coming—indeed of the already in-breaking—rule of God. . .' From the point of view of the kerygma, on the other hand, 'the decisive eschatological event has already taken place.' The distinction is drawn more finely *ibid*., 26: 'All efforts to show that the historical Jesus already saw in his work the onset of the time of salvation, are not able to obscure the fundamental difference between his proclamation and the kerygma of Christ. . .' It is simply not possible 'to project'

such verses as II Cor. 5.17, John 12.31 etc. 'into the proclamation of the historical Jesus.' One does well to remember that Bultmann does not deny that 'existential interpretation can rediscover the meaning of such sayings in the sayings and actions of the historical Jesus', even if he says that in this one is 'in fact led to this interpretation by the kerygma.' This reminds us of the talk of 'implicit and explicit' which is so important in Bultmann's attempts to define the difference between the two. For this see above pp. 69*f*. *This schema is different from the schema of eschatological phases in time*, which seems to gain the upper hand in Bultmann's work in the end. Cf. the final quotation from Reginald H. Fuller, SAH 1960, 3; 27: '. . . Easter discloses the achievement of a further phase of God's eschatological action. . .'

49 Cf. E. Käsemann, 'Die Anfänge christlicher Theologie'. ZThK 57, 1960, 162-85, and the contributions to this discussion by E. Fuchs and myself: ZThK 58, 1961, 226-67, and particularly E. Fuchs' essay, *'Das Zeitverständnis Jesu'*. In: E. Fuchs, *Ges. Aufs.* II, 1960, 304-76. Also: E. Käsemann, 'Gottesgerechtigkeit bei Paulus'. ZThK 58, 1961, 367-78.

50 When Bultmann says of the kerygma in SAH 1960, 3; 26 (see also 23) that faith is 'faith in Jesus Christ, which was not demanded by the historical Jesus. It is only now that there can be such faith,' this is naturally an accurate description of the external facts of the matter. Yet I would question the understanding of faith which seems to lie behind it and which suggests that the kerygma supplemented or outdid the faith which Jesus preached by another faith. Yet if both cases really are concerned with faith—and that means with God!—then the difference can only lie in the way in which the ground of faith is made explicit. Cf. my essays: 'Was heisst Glauben?' SgV 216, 1958. 'Jesus und Glaube'. WuG 203-54=E. T. 'Jesus and Faith'. WaF 200-46. Also: WuG 315*ff*=WaF 302*ff*.

51 SAH 1960, 3; 13*f*: 'First it must be made clear that this "introductory" investigation, that is, the historical critical analysis of the Synoptic Gospels, is relevant only to the question of the objectively ascertainable history of Jesus. Here it can indeed allay doubts cast on the historicity of Jesus, which is asserted in the That of the kerygma; it can further give an indication of the nature of the historical person of Jesus with some degree of accuracy.' Yet this sort of illustration of the That by the What and the How is really superfluous, says Bultmann.

52 *Ibid.*, 9. Although in fact he puts this in such a way that he still leaves the problem unanswered in spite of the historical argument: 'Paul and John have both shown in their different ways that one does not *need* to go beyond the That.' All that remains is a certain room for play for things which are superfluous yet not forbidden. 'The decisive thing is simply the That.'

53 See above pp. 130*ff*. The question of the theological motive behind the formation of the Gospels.

54 See above p. 36, *n*. 2, and below pp. 118*f*.

55 Cf. Bultmann's early essay: 'Welchen Sinn hat es, von Gott zu reden?' GuV 1, 26-37.

56 SAH 1960, 3; 9.

57 His formulation with regard to Paul is characteristic of this view, *ibid*. 9: '. . . his kerygma requires of the life of Jesus only the fact *that* [!] he lived and was crucified.'

58 GuV 1, 273: 'There is no doubt that he [Jesus] thought of himself as the preacher of the Word.' Cf. the stereotyped formulations of the problem, e.g. SAH 1960, 3; 23: 'Why did the preacher have to become the one who was preached?'

59 SAH 1960, 3; 15.

60 *Ibid.*, 16.

61 He has been using this formula since 1929. GuV 1, 174: 'Jesus gave no express teaching *about his own person*. On the other hand, he stressed the importance and the decisiveness of the fact of his own person, because he is the bearer of the Word in the last decisive hour, and because this means that it happens *that* here and now his Word impinges on the listener.' '. . . in the call to decision to men confronted by his person, there is contained implicitly a "Christology", but Jesus does not develop it. *If* it is to be developed then the point of this Christology can only be that it implements the decision for or against him . . .' Similarly, 204*f* 266. TheolNT 44=E.T. 1, 43.

62 SAH 1960, 3; 17: 'But how far does all this take us? It certainly enables us to understand the historical continuity between the work of Jesus and the kerygma . . .' Then follows the sentence quoted above. The same view is to be found in GuV 1, 205 and particularly 266: 'If the primitive community calls him Messiah, then it shows in its own way that it has understood him. The great riddle of the New Testament,

how the proclaimer became the one who was proclaimed, why the community proclaimed not only the ideas of his preaching, but also and indeed principally proclaimed him himself, why moreover Paul and John as good as completely ignore the content of his preaching, this great riddle is solved as soon as one sees that it is the That of his proclamation which is decisive . . . The proclaimer had to become the one who was proclaimed because the decisive thing was the That of his proclamation, his person, not his personality, its here and now, its event, its commission, its appeal. By calling him the Messiah the primitive community sees him as the decisive event, as the act of God which brings in the new world.'

63 *Ibid.*, 17.

64 *Ibid.*, 17.

65 *Ibid.*, 17. See above p. 70, n. 62. Cf. *ibid.*, 14: Historical criticism can indeed 'allay doubts cast on the historicity of Jesus, which is asserted in the That of the kerygma;' but it is not able 'to afford a proof that the historical continuity between Jesus and the kerygma is in the nature of a material agreement'.

66 *Ibid.*, 23.

67 This in indicated by the remarks which follow the two quotations above, according to which, historical criticism can determine the continuity but not the material unity (or rather agreement): see above *n.* 63 and 65.

68 *Op. cit.*, 17: 'Does the eschatological consciousness of Jesus impart an eschatological self-understanding to those who observe it as an historical phenomenon?'

69 GuV 1, 266. See above p. 70, *n.* 62.

70 Bultmann draws a sharp line between this attempt to interpret the 'matter' after the manner of existential interpretation, and objectifying critical historical research (cf. what he says about 'the two ways of interpreting the life of Jesus', *ibid.*, 15 as well as 18 and 23). He then goes on remarkably to equate existential interpretation with 'existential encounter' (*existentiell*) in such a way that the problem of the rivalry between the proclamation of Jesus and the kerygma has to be raised. Cf. above p. 58, *n.* 14 and 15 and p. 62, *n.* 33.

71 Bultmann actually says 'prove' (*ibid.*, 14. 17), because he is immediately concerned with the theological abuse of historical work.

72 Guv I, 174, 204*f*, 266. See above p. 70, *n*. 61 and 62.

73 I would again draw attention to his formulations in GuV I, 266. See above p. 78, *n*. 62.

74 GuV I, 205: 'Christology in the primitive community had become explicit enough for them to confess that Jesus had been made the Messiah by God and that he would come as such. This shows that they saw his Word and by this is meant not the timeless ideas which it contained, but the fact that it was spoken by him and that they were addressed by him—as the decisive act of God. Yet this means that the retailing of the preaching of Jesus could not take the form of a mere reproduction of his ideas, but that the preacher must become the one who was proclaimed. The That of his proclamation is the really decisive thing.' SAH 1960, 3; 23: 'If the proclamation of Jesus (and his life) force the listener to make a decision and open up to him the possibility of a new existence—why is it that the apostolic preaching cannot content itself with merely *repeating* the proclamation of Jesus, in the way that other pupils repeat the teaching of their master?'

75 The connection with the question of authority is suggested e.g. in GuV I, 205: 'The What of his proclamation is not in the least impugned by his death on the cross; what is impugned is his credentials for preaching, the That, the fact that it is the one who is God's messenger who brings the ultimate, decisive Word.' Yet we must be clear that the 'credentials', i.e. his authority, are not something extra over and above his proclamation, but are rather identical with the matter with which the proclamation of Jesus is concerned. Similarly the That is not *brutum factum* but the fact of *Word*, which is to say the word-event in its full power; that is to say in the power which comes to the Word as Word, i.e. as true Word (and this means God's Word).

76 See above p. 58, *n*. 18. GuV I, 289*f*: 'If the Christ event is continued in the proclamation of the Word, if Christ is present in the Word of the church, then everything drives us to the assertion *that he himself is the Word* . . .' Similarly, 292. GuV II, 261: '. . . he is the Word and as such he is God. . .'

77 See above p. 42, *n*. 36.

78 The purpose of this necessary distinction is not to separate the two terms from each other, but to further a proper understanding of their relationship.

79 Cf. GuV 1, 205. I have kept to Bultmann's terminology although I am of the opinion that the concept of the call to decision is inadequate for the purpose of characterising the word event, which is identical with Jesus himself.

80 E.g. GuV 1, 204.

81 SAH 1960, 3; 8.

82 It is admittedly a pure hypothesis, yet in so far as this sort of thing is permissible with regard to historical questions, I would make the following suggestion. I doubt whether it would in the long run have been possible to have handed down the Pauline kerygma in the form which we know it, without giving it a more concrete relation to Jesus. Without the Gospels (this is scarcely conceivable) it would have been unintelligible to us in its character as kerygma of Christ.

83 See above pp. 53*f*.

84 This corresponds to the step which we envisaged above, p. 66.

85 Behind these remarks lies a good deal of thought about the theology of W. Herrmann, among others. The distinction which he makes between the basis and the content of faith, which recently has been much discussed and more often than not misunderstood, seems to me too important to be discussed in a note here. I hope to go into this in a later publication where I shall also deal with the accusation levelled against me on the basis of my article in ZThK 57, 1960, 318-56, 'Die Evidenz des Ethischen und die Theologie', of 'having reintroduced Herrmann's ideas'—was 'Herrmann's theological work . . . out of date even at the time it was written'? Cf. W. Pannenberg, 'Die Krise des Ethischen und die Theologie, ThLZ 87, 1962, 7-16, esp. 12. For an indication of how to approach the question of the basis of faith, cf. W. Herrmann, *Die Gewissheit des Glaubens und die Freiheit der Theologie*, 1889², 14*f*: 'Christianity does not fall into every soul from heaven; it is planted into the historical life of mankind. Even mere continued activity in this historical movement does not in itself make us christians. Before we can say this we shall have to venture our life on certain historical facts. No one can do that and at the same time question those facts as an historian must do. This difficulty has caused increasing unease in the Evangelical Church since the 18th century. The attempts to get round it have played the most important role in church history since that time. Large circles of the church prefer to

think only of *an historical cause of the church, a ground of faith*, in which we must place our trust in the present. On the other hand it is understandable enough if another group, full of enthusiastic love for the historical saviour, should repudiate historical research with great determination, or, which is just as immoral, should secure or suppress certain historical judgments by means of ecclesiastical agitation. The struggle between these two groups completely fills the public life of the church. Yet the warriors are beginning to tire. The signs are growing that people are turning to a theology which instead of trying to hack the knot to pieces is concerned to disentangle it.'

86 SAH 1960, 3; 25.

87 Cf. the continuation of the quotation *ibid.*, 17 (see above p. 71, *n.* 68): 'Yet this is precisely the intention of the kerygma which as such claims to be an eschatological event . . . which in direct address promises life and death . . . Does Jesus' claim to authority, seen as an historical phenomenon, extend beyond the time of his earthly work? Do the call and promises of the historical Jesus, with all their "directness" reach out to later generations? This is indeed what happens in the kerygma, in which it is not the *historical* Jesus, but the *exalted* Jesus, who says: *edothē moi pasa exousia.* The Christ of the kerygma has, as it were, crowded out the historical Jesus, and now addresses the hearer—every hearer—in full authority. How then can we speak of an identity between the work of Jesus and the kerygma, in the sense that in Jesus' words and deeds the kerygma is contained *in nuce*?'

88 *Ibid.*, 26: 'If then it is true that the kerygma proclaims Jesus as the Christ, as the eschatological event, that the kerygma claims that Christ is present in its proclamation, then it has put itself in the place of the historical Jesus; it represents him.'

89 The invocation of Jesus should in truth be understood in the sense of *auctoritas causativa* which points us towards the eschatological self-understanding—which is of course faith!—and only so makes eschatological proclamation as such (and not an historical phenomenon) intelligible.

90 See the previous note and *op. cit.*, 27: 'If it is true that the church in its kerygma represents the historical Jesus, if faith in Christ is at the same time faith in the church, or faith in the Holy Spirit, which it has received as a gift after Easter . . . then we can say that

faith in the church as bearer of the kerygma *is* the Easter faith, the faith that Jesus Christ is present in the kerygma.' Yet the assertion, *ibid.*, 26: 'It is clear that "church" is seen here not as an institution but as an eschatological event,' does not really dissipate the dangers which lurk in the ambiguous phrases, 'take the place of' and 'represent'. What is meant by saying that the authority of the church is only the authority of Jesus in that it invokes the authority of Jesus and not its own authority?

91 *Ibid.*, 27: 'The statement that Jesus rose into the kerygma means that Jesus is really present in the kerygma, that it is *his* Word which meets the hearer in the kerygma.'

92 Cf. WA 7; 742, 13-16 (Ad librum . . . Magistri Ambrosii Catharini . . . responsio, 1521): A representative represents a ruler when he is absent; therefore wherever a representative of God rules, there is no God. For where God is present there is no need of a representative, but rather of ministers, just as the apostles called themselves not representatives but ministers of God.

93 See pp. 83*f*.

CHAPTER IV

Towards a Christology

1 Cf. *Christian Discourses*, tr. Lowrie, p. 77.

2 Cf. P. Tillich's *Das Wesen und Wandel des Glaubens*, the revised German edition of *The Dynamics of Faith*. Trs.

3 WA 40, 1; 524, 11*ff*. (Gal. 1531). Cf. WuG 292 = WaF 280.

4 See above p. 28, *n*. 8.

CHAPTER V

Towards an ecclesiology

1 Cf. my essay: 'Das Grund-Geschehen von Kirche'. MPTh 51, 1962, 1-4.

2 A. Loisy: *L'Évangile et l'Église*, Paris 1902, 111: *'Jésus annonçait le royaume, et c'est l'Église qui est venue.'*

3 WA 18; 310, 10*f.* = Clem 3; 56, 37*f.* (*Ermahnung zum Frieden . . .* 1525).

4 WA 10, 3; 15, 10 = Clem 7; 368, 18 (*Invocavit-Predigten* 1522).

5 WA 50; 250, 3-5 = Clem 4; 318, 32*f.* = BSLK 459, 21*f.* (*Schmalk. Art.* 1536).

6 Cf. *The Nature of Faith*: Chapter 14, *passim*. Trs.

CHAPTER VI

Appendix

1 See p. 20, *n.* 13.

2 *Kurze Darstellung des theologischen Studiums*, 1830². ed. H. Scholz, 1935, para. 1; E.T. 'A Short Introduction to Theological Study', 1850, W. Farrer.

3 *Idem.*, para. 1.

4 *Idem.*, para. 3*ff.*

5 Cf. Fr. Kluge, *Etymologisches Wörterbuch der deutschen Sprache*, ed. A. Götze, 1943¹²·¹³ s.v.

6 See p. 27, *n.* 5.

7 G. Gloege in RGG³ II, 225.

8 As, e.g. KD I, I, 1932, 283 = E.T. I, I, 1936, p. 307. E. Brunner, *Die christliche Lehre von Gott. Dogmatik I*, 1946, 113 = *The Christian Doctrine of God*, 1949, p. 112*f.* P. Althaus, *Die christliche Wahrheit. Lehrbuch der Dogmatik*, 1952³, 243.

9 Nietzsche I, 1961, 92.

10 O. Ritschl, 'Das Wort dogmaticus in der Geschichte des Sprachgebrauchs bis zum Aufkommen des Ausdrucks theologia dogmatica'. FJK, 1920, 260-72. See also O. Ritschl *Dogmengeschichte des Protestantismus*, I, 1908, 14-36. E. Rothacker, 'Die dogmatische Denkform in den Geisteswissenschaften und das Problem des Historismus', AAMz 1954, 243-98. For the history of the word 'dogma' see particularly A. Deneffe, 'Dogma, Wort und Begriff'. In: *Scholastik* 6, 1931, 381-400, 505-38. J. Ranft and E. Fascher in RAC III, 1257-60 IV, 1-24.

11 FJK, 261.

12 References in Liddell-Scott, s.v.

13 M. Pohlenz, *Die Stoa*, I (1948), 1959², 333*f*, II (1949), 1955², 164.

14 O. Ritschl: FJK, 260.

15 See J. Wallmann, *Der Theologiebegriff bei Johann Gerhard und Georg Calixt* BHTh 30, 1961, 153f.

16 Cf. part of a passage quoted by O. Ritschl, *Dogmengeschichte des Protestantismus*, I, 31: *Opposita utique sunt dogmatica et historica; at non subjecto, sed modo; non re considerata, sed forma considerandi.*

17 *Eth. Nich.*, 1103a, 5.

18 E.g. the division of the contents of the Bible into '*historica*' and '*dogmatica*' in Johann Gerhard's *Loci theol.*, I, 170.

19 See p. 36, *n.* I.

20 'Kerygma und Tradition in der Hermeneutik Adolf Schlatters', in: *Arbeitsgemeinschaft für Forschung des Landes Nordrhein-Westfalen. Geisteswissenschaften*, H. 45, 1955, 13*f*. Incidentally, with regard to the title of this paper, Schlatter, as far as I know, scarcely ever uses the word kerygma.

21 'Der KERYGMA-Begriff in der ältesten christlichen Literatur. Zur Frage neuer theologischer Begriffsbildungen', ZNW 48, 1957, 77-101, esp. 77-9.

22 RGG[3] III, 1250-4.

23 J. S. Semler: *Versuch einer freien theologischen Lehrart*, 1777, 5.

24 E.g. in *Abhandlung von freier Untersuchung des Canon*, IV, 74.

25 *Ibid.*, 90.

26 Cf. WuG 327*f*. = WaF 312*f*.

27 E.g. in *Axiomata* . . . and *Nöthige Antwort* . . .

28 *Sämtliche Werke*, ed. B. Sulphan, vol. 19, 1880, 382.

29 As e.g. Fr. D. E. Schleiermacher, *Der christliche Glaube*, 1830[2], para. 15, 2. Cf. para. 18, 1, 3 = E.T., *The Christian Faith*, 1928.

30 E.g. K. G. Bretschneider, *Handbuch der Dogmatik der evangelisch-lutherischen Kirche*, I, 1838[4], 23-9.

31 Cf. the term which was coined for this distinction '*Keryktik*': R. E. Stier, *Grundriss einer biblischen Keryktik*, 1830; here we may notice too the surprisingly infrequent use of the word by M. Kähler, which he uses to refer to the preaching which establishes the church, e.g. *Der sogenannte historische Jesus und der geschichtliche, biblische Christus*, 1896[2], 26.

32 Cf. e.g. the admittedly very specialised use of the concept of kerygma in A. von Harnack's *Lehrbuch der Dogmengeschichte*, I,

1931[5], 178*f.* = E.T., *History of Dogma*, vol. I, 1894; Harnack's *Die Mission und Ausbreitung des Christentums in den ersten drei Jahrhunderten*, I, 1924[4], 120*ff.*; also, the use of the concept in the strict sense of kerygma of Christ for which he invokes Irenaeus' distinction between *pistis* and *kērygma* in J. Haussleiter, *Trinitarischer Glaube und Christusbekenntnis in der alten Kirche*, BFChTh 25, 4, 1920.

33 In M. Dibelius's *Die Formgeschichte des Evangeliums*, 1919, 4-15; see too here R. Bultmann, RGG[2] III, 1682; cf. E. Fascher, 'Die formgeschichtliche Methode. Eine Darstellung und Kritik', ZNW Supp. 2, 1924, esp. 214 n. 1: a somewhat poor argument from the differences among the form-critics.

34 Cf. here H. Ott in RGG[3] III, 1251*ff.*

35 = 1931[2], 297*f.* = E.T., *The History of the Synoptic Tradition*, 1963, 275.

36 GuV I, 153*ff.*, esp. 172-87.

37 SgV 135, 1929, 28, 44 = GuV III, 20, 34 = E.T., *Existence and Faith. The Concept of Revelation in the New Testament*, 77, 90. 'Die Bedeutung des geschichtlichen Jesus für die Theologie des Paulus', GuV I, 188*ff*, esp. 208. Article: 'Paulus' in RGG[2] IV, 1019*ff*, esp. 1027*ff*.

38 See above p. 39, *n*. 14.

39 See above p. 46, *n*. 45.

40 EvTh 8, 1948/9, 462-73; reprinted in H. Schlier, *Die Zeit der Kirche*, 1958[2], 147-59.

41 EvTh 10, 1950/51, 481-507; reprinted in *Die Zeit der Kirche*, 206-32.

42 Vol. II: *Dogmatik*, 1955, 40-9, 98-101 = E.T., *Dogmatics*, 1959, 41*ff*, 107*ff*.

43 KuD 3, 1957, 77-108.

44 ThEx NF 94, 1961, esp. 13*ff*, 24*f*, 30*f*.

45 EvTh 10, 1950/1, 490 = 214.

46 *Idem.*, 493 = 217.

47 *Idem.*, 491*f*. = 216.

48 *Idem.*, 492*f*. = 216*f*.

49 *Idem.*, 506 = 230*f*.

50 *Idem.*, 507 = 232.

51 *Idem.*, 507 = 232.

52 *Idem.*, 502 = 227.

53 *Idem.*, 494 = 218.
54 Cf. WuG 319*ff* = WaF 305*ff*.
55 EvTh 10, 505*f*. = 230.
56 See p. 58, n. 16.
57 Cf. my book, *Das Wesen des christlichen Glaubens* (1959), 1961[4], 48*ff*, 66*ff* = E.T., *The Nature of Faith*, 1961, 44*ff*, 58*ff*. WuG 203-54; 300-18 = WaF 201-46, 288-304.
58 SAH 1960, 3; 19*f*.
59 Cf. Fr. D. E. Schleiermacher, *Hermeneutik und Kritik mit besonderer Beziehung auf das Neue Testament*, ed. Fr. Lücke, 1838, 13, 143*ff*. Fr. D. E. Schleiermacher, 'Hermeneutik. Nach den Handschriften neu herausgegeben und eingeleitet von H. Kimmerle, AAH 1952, 2; 81, 165*f*.
60 SAH 1960, 3; 12.
61 E. Fuchs, *Ges. Aufs.* II, 298, cf. the general context of these remarks, 294*ff*.
62 Cf. on this point the earlier remarks of P. Biehl, 'Zur Frage nach dem historischen Jesus'. ThR NF 24, 1957/8, 54-76. Commenting on a remark of E. Fuchs, ZThK 53, 1956, 222 = *Ges. Aufs.* II, 157, P. Biehl (*op. cit.*, p. 76) asks: 'Where is the *existential* basis of the hermeneutic insight that one can infer from the demands which Jesus made to what he actually did himself?'
63 SAH 1960, 3; 19.
64 *Ibid.*, 20.
65 *Ibid.*, 19.
66 SAH 1960, 3; 11*f* and see above p. 57, *n*. 9.
67 *Ibid.*, 19.
68 *Ibid.*, 20.
69 See above p. 58, *n*. 14 and 15.
70 SAH 1960, 3; 19.
71 See above p. 37, *n*. 7.
72 Cf. pp. 94*ff*.
73 SAH 1960, 3; 20.
74 See above pp. 23*f* and esp. *n*. 3.
75 SAH 1960, 3; 20.
76 ZThK 55, 1958, 97 = WuG 240 = WaF 234.
77 For Luther's occasional remarks on this scholastic view in the first lectures on the Psalms, see WA 4; 266, 24*ff*, 519, 33*f*, cf. R.

Schwarz, *Fides, Spes und Caritas beim jungen Luther. Unter besonderer Berücksichtigung der mittelalterlichen Tradition*, AKG 34, 1962, 233*f*, *n*. 527.

78 Cf. WuG 308 = WaF 295*f*.

79 ZThK Supp. 1, 1959, 22*f* = WuG 309*f*=WaF 296*f*; cf. SAH 1960, 3; 20, n. 49.

80 See p. 67, *n*. 53.

81 Cf. W. Wrede.

82 ZThK 54, 1957, 277-96.

83 *Op. cit*., 293f.

84 Conzelmann, *op. cit*., 295.

85 G. Bornkamm, in the article: 'Evangelien, formgeschichtlich', RGG[3] II, 749. Bultmann had already pointed to this in his *Die Geschichte der synoptischen Tradition*, 1931[2], 396 = E.T., 371; see above p. 116.

86 Conzelmann, *op. cit*., 295.

87 Cf. the further discussion of these points in E. Fuchs, 'Das Neue Testament und das hermeneutsiche Problem', ZThK 58, 1961, 198-226, esp. 201.

Index

Index

(*a*=Appendix; *n*=Notes)

Index

Index